Two Screenplays

LUCHINO VISCONTI

TWO SCREENPLAYS

La Terra Trema
Senso

Translated from the Italian by Judith Green

The Orion Press   New York   1970

CONTENTS

La Terra Trema (1947)

Credits

Producer:	Salvo d'Angelo
Production Manager:	Anna Davini
Director:	Luchino Visconti
Assistant Directors:	Francesco Rosi, Franco Zeffirelli
Screenplay:	Luchino Visconti
Director of Photography:	G. R. Aldo
Camera Operator:	Gianni di Venanzo
Editor:	Mario Serandrei
Music:	Willi Ferroro
Sound:	Vittorio Trentino

The cast is composed of the people of a small fishing village in Sicily.

Village square. Dawn.

As the church bells ring, some figures are seen coming out of a lighted doorway and entering the church. Someone is whistling. Voices are calling out, at first indistinguishably, then:

VOICE: Raimondo! Raimondo! Hurry up; it's dawn!

ANOTHER VOICE: Lorenzo! Can you see the boats?

VOICE: Yes, out past the rocks.

Other figures approach and stop to look out to sea.

Beach. Dawn.

The church and some of the village houses stand at the edge of the beach. A group of men (the fish dealers) walk out toward the harbor. The boats are seen passing the two great rocks guarding the little port as they return from the night's fishing. Shouts and cries between the sea and the beach. The church bells are ringing.

RAIMONDO: Uncle Giovanni Sigaretta, have you caught anything?

LORENZO: Can I bring the scales?

SIGARETTA *(from the sea)*: We've got a lot. You can bring the scales.

NINO: Hey you, Angelo Malaterra, have you caught anything?

ANGELO: Not much, not much.

NINO: You never do get much.

ANGELO: It's God's will.

VOICE: What do you guys want?

ANOTHER VOICE: Don't sell your fish before we get there.

The dealers talk and shout among themselves.

Courtyard of the Valastro house. Dawn.

The church bells are still ringing and continue throughout the scene. Mara, carrying a lamp, goes toward the entrance. She opens the courtyard door, looks outside, and then goes back into the house.

Valastro house. Dining room. Dawn.

Mara's lamp lights up the room as she enters. She sets it down on the table and goes to open the window, then returns to the table. It is getting light outside; Mara blows out the lamp and goes to open another window.

MARA: Lucia! Hurry up; you've got to get the bread from the baker's.

Lucia runs into the room and goes over to the sideboard. She takes out a rag and begins to dust the furniture.

LUCIA: Wait, I'll clean up here and then I'll go!

MARA: Lia! *(Mara is now sweeping the floor.)* Lia! Lia, come here and throw some water on the floor! *(Little Lia runs in, takes the basin from the top of the sideboard and begins to splash water over the floor as Mara continues to sweep.)* Over here... over here...

Lucia finishes dusting, then goes to the sideboard. Mara continues to sweep as Lia leans against the table watching her sisters. Lucia gazes ecstatically at the family portrait hanging on the wall.

MARA: Lucia, what are you looking at?

LUCIA: At our brothers: when they're at sea I always think

about them. I think about that morning when we were waiting for our father and he never came back.

Mara looks toward the window.

MARA: They'll be back soon. *(Then, putting away the broom, she comes over to Lucia.)* Fix your hair, Lucia. Wait, I'll help you put on your kerchief.

Mara ties her sister's hair back with a kerchief.

LUCIA: You remember that day we went to Catania to have our picture taken? It seems like yesterday!

The mother enters the room with the baby girl in her arms. A cock crows. Lucia points out the people in the photograph one by one.

LUCIA: Look at Antonio in his navy uniform, when he'd just gotten out of the service...Cola...and Vanni—he was wearing long pants for the first time...Alfio...Grandfather...

MARA: They're all sailors!

LUCIA: The sea is bitter!

Beach. Dawn.

The fishermen have just landed their boats and are gathering up the nets. Antonio and his brothers are beside their boat. Vanni calls to Antonio, who answers him with a shout. Shouts, calls, questions and answers—all indistinguishable—continue to ring out throughout the scene.

VANNI: Cola, can you hear me? Where's Grandfather?

ANTONIO: Go on. He's gone home already. What are you two doing?

Antonio removes his wool cap as he speaks to his brothers. The beach is filled with fishing boats and men crowding about them. The Valastro men carry their net across the harbor of Aci Trezza. The horizon is beginning to lighten out beyond the rocks. The fishermen move around on the beach and begin to bargain with the dealers.

Beach. Day.

The fishermen are mending their nets. The Valastros carry their nets along the beach and spread them out on the ground. Cola, already seated beside Antonio and some other fishermen, begins to mend a net. One of the other fishermen calls out.

FISHERMAN: Hey, Maccherone, get me the big needle in the basket on the boat!

COLA: Maccherone, bring all the stuff here; everything's wrecked this morning and there's a lot to mend!

ANTONIO: Bring the jug of water too!

MACCHERONE: Hey, I can't bring everything, I only have two hands!

Bandiera and another fisherman talk as they mend the nets of another boat.

BANDIERA: See? That's what happens when you treat kids too well. Did you hear how they answer back?

SECOND FISHERMAN: I told you you shouldn't treat kids so well when you're at sea!

COLA: Everything's broken up this morning; there's enough mending to last us a month!

ANTONIO: A month, no, just a week.

One of the fishermen in the background calls out.

THIRD FISHERMAN: What a bad night: ours is all wrecked too.

Antonio interrupts his work and turns to the others:

ANTONIO: You think our "friends" care about these things? The hell they do! We're just a bunch of draft animals to them, good only as long as we work.

BANDIERA: They sure get down here early in the morning to wait for us to bring in the fish!

ANTONIO: If we could manage it, it would be worth our while to take the fish to Catania, instead of slaving for those guys.

COLA: Did you hear Raimondo and Nino Nasca fighting this morning on the pier? Raimondo said he'd bought our catch!

FIRST FISHERMAN: Don't think those guys ever really fight, Cola; they just put on a show to make themselves look good. They argue, they fight, but they're always on the same side, against us!

ANTONIO *(increasingly excited)*: We're the ones who're always fighting each other. Because everybody's looking out for their own interest... and we'd sell our souls for a penny!

COLA *(sad and thoughtful)*: Things should be different!

Beach. Day.

A group of fishermen and dealers are arguing excitedly. Maccherone seems to be looking for something as he walks among the groups of men discussing the price of the fish. The talk and the shouts are indistinguishable except for some numbers:

MEN: ...eighty... eighty-five... sixty... sixty-five... four hundred... four thirty-five... five hundred...

Bastianello Alley. Day.

A boy is selling tangerines.

BOY: Tangerines, tangerines! Sweet as honey! Tangerines!

Lucia comes out of her house to buy some tangerines. Another woman appears, combing her hair, and then still another, with one child in her arms and another hanging on to her dress. They discuss the price of the tangerines with the boy. Some indistinguishable phrases, then:

WOMAN: Hey you, how much are you asking for your tangerines?

BOY: Twenty lire.

WOMAN: That's too much. Who'd buy them at that price?

The men come up from the sea, carrying their nets on their shoulders.

ALFIO: Tangerines!

LUCIA: Hi, Antonio. Hi, Cola.

ANTONIO: Hi, Lucia.

COLA: Hi, Lucia, what're you buying?

Courtyard of Valastro house. Day.

The men pass into the courtyard, carrying their nets and talking among themselves. Lucia enters carrying the tangerines in her apron. Lia runs up to her and takes one.

LUCIA: Don't take them all!

Mara is sweeping in front of the house.

MARA: Lucia, come help me.

LUCIA: I'll be right there, Mara, I've bought a kilo of tangerines.

Lia and Lucia go into the house. The mother comes out of the kitchen door carrying the baby.

MOTHER: Did the men come back yet?

MARA: Yes, Mother.

The Valastro brothers and Maccherone pass her on their way into the house.

ANTONIO: Bless me, Mother.

MOTHER: God bless you.

MACCHERONE: Antonio, I can't find the baling scoop.

COLA: Bless me, Mother.

Valastro house. Dining room. Day.

Antonio, Mara, Alfio, and Maccherone enter the dining room. Alfio picks up a loaf of bread from the table.

COLA: Alfio, don't touch the bread; wait for Mother to give it to you.

ANTONIO: Here's Grandfather.

MACCHERONE: I looked for it all over the place but I couldn't find it.

ANTONIO: Don't tell me. Go back and look for it again.

MACCHERONE: We must have lost it at sea during the night.

MARA: Lucia, where's Grandfather's cap?

Mara goes out into the courtyard, followed by Maccherone.

LUCIA: There it is, on the seat.

The grandfather enters, takes his cap and goes into the men's bedroom with the boys.

Men's bedroom. Day.

Antonio tosses his cap on the clothes rack and sits down on the bed to take off his boots. The grandfather and the two boys begin to undress.

COLA: Grandfather, how much did we make today? Fifteen thousand five hundred, right?

GRANDFATHER: We had ten kilos of palamiti and not much else. We got seven thousand seven fifty.

ANTONIO: The usual thing: we slave all night long and the others catch our fish!

The grandfather has the money in his lap.

GRANDFATHER: It's been that way since I can remember. At Trezza, at Castello, at Cape Mulini...

Antonio suddenly jumps up.

ANTONIO: It can't go on this way! *(He goes to the door and calls his sister.)* Lucia, bring me the jug of water so I can wash my face. *(Then he goes into the next room.)* We can't go on like this! I've told you so many times, Grandfather!

GRANDFATHER: Cola, what's the matter with Antonio?

COLA: Grandfather, you know what's the matter? Antonio's been on the mainland, when he was in the navy, and he can't stand to see this injustice any more. He doesn't think like us any more, he thinks a different way. Isn't that right, Antonio?

GRANDFATHER *(waving the money)*: I'm seventy years old and I've always thought the same way and everything's turned out all right. Antonio has to listen to the old people, because the old proverb says: "Muscles of the young and brains of the old!"

Lucia and Mara enter with the jugs of water and the basins, which they set down on the chairs.

LUCIA: Grandfather, don't get so excited. *(She carries a jug to Antonio.)* Antonio, here's your water.

Mara helps her grandfather and brothers.

MARA: Come get washed, Vanni.

Lucia goes to help Alfio.

LUCIA: Hurry up, Alfio.

ANTONIO *(singing)*: I die without you... I die without yooou...

Vanni goes to wash.

Room adjoining men's bedroom. Day.

Cola washes, bending over the basin.

COLA: Antonio, you've upset Grandfather now; you shouldn't talk to him about these things.

ANTONIO *(soaping himself)*: Poor Grandfather, he's still so old-fashioned! *(Singing)* My treacherous love, my looove!... You didn't become a holy nun...

COLA: Antonio, when you sing that song you're thinking about that girl in Via Ferretta, eh?

ANTONIO *(laughing)*: The fish in the sea are born for who's hungry!

Cola and Antonio laugh as they dry their faces. Mara enters to empty two basins of water. The three then go back into the bedroom, where the grandfather is sitting on the big bed. Antonio puts on his boots and gets ready to go out.

Men's bedroom. Day.

Antonio takes his cap and says goodbye to his grandfather.

ANTONIO: Grandfather, I'm going out. Take it easy.

GRANDFATHER: Where're you going? Don't you want your money?

ANTONIO: Give my share to my mother.

He goes out. Cola, whistling, goes to the back of the room. Alfio is lying in the big bed where the grandfather is dividing the money into equal shares. Maccherone enters and goes toward the bed.

MACCHERONE: Holy Saint John, the scoop's lost!

GRANDFATHER: You boys lose everything!

The boys crowd around the bed as Mara puts the grandfather's slippers on. Cola is combing his hair.

COLA: Grandfather, Antonio's going fishing!

GRANDFATHER: Didn't we catch enough for you? Come here,

boys, let's reckon up. Seven thousand seven hundred and fifty lire, divided by fifteen, makes five hundred apiece.

ALFIO: How about me?

GRANDFATHER: Two-fifty because you're little.

Cola and Vanni take their shares.

COLA: I'm taking mine and Antonio's.

VANNI: And I'm taking mine.

Outside Nedda's house. Day.

Smoking a cigarette, Antonio walks rapidly uphill along a path. As he reaches the house, he stops and tosses away his cigarette.

ANTONIO: Nedda! *(Nedda, carrying two rabbits by their ears, turns and smiles; Antonio smiles back.)* I wish I was one of those rabbits you take such good care of!

He approaches her, smiling. Nedda sits down on a little wall.

NEDDA: Of course I take good care of them! Because rabbits aren't naughty... *(She hands him one of the rabbits, which he takes and caresses.)* ...like men!

ANTONIO: You know I'm not naughty, Nedda; you know I love you so much!

NEDDA *(laughing)*: Yes, yes, I know. You've told me so many times, Antonio! But don't worry... *(She rises and runs away; Antonio follows her; she turns toward him.)* ...when the right time comes I'll find me a husband!

Nedda runs behind the house toward the rabbit hutch. Antonio hands her the second rabbit to put back in the hutch.

ANTONIO: You're a special kind of girl! I know your family wants you to marry a rich man!

Nedda smiles, her hands behind her back.

NEDDA: Rich or poor, he's got to please me!

The couple strolls off.

ANTONIO: But remember one thing, Nedda, a man who's rich today may be poor tomorrow. *(They stop beside a tree; Nedda leans against it.)* And a man who's poor today, if he's got something up here *(Touching his forehead)*, can be rich tomorrow!

Nedda laughs and turns toward Antonio, who gazes wordlessly at her.

NEDDA: Then we'll talk about it tomorrow, Antonio!

Street before the headquarters of the Treasury Guards. Day.

The sergeant, Don Salvatore, lights a cigarette as he stands at the rail and watches Lucia walking up the road. A corporal greets him with a slap on the shoulder.

CORPORAL: You keep yourself busy, sergeant!

DON SALVATORE: I have to! Since there're so many pretty girls in Trezza.

Two guards are talking in the street. A woman, Giovannina, comes along in the direction opposite to Lucia's, greeting first the women mending nets before their houses...

GIOVANNINA: Hello, ladies! *(Then the guards)* Good morning, fellows! *(And finally Don Salvatore)* Good day, sergeant!

DON SALVATORE: Good day, Giovannina!

As Giovannina continues on her way, the sergeant—still watching Lucia— throws away his cigarette, buckles on his service belt, and gets ready to go out.

Valastro house. Dining room. Toward evening.

Alfio, holding a box full of bottles, smiles at Mara, who is pouring wine from a large bottle into smaller ones. Lucia, Lia, and the mother are preparing a supper of bread and anchovies for the men. Vanni walks across the room, and Alfio follows him with the box after Mara has given him the last bottle. Lucia leaves the table and comes over to Mara. Antonio and then Cola cross the room. The two sisters and the mother carry the food and a bottle of wine toward the courtyard.

Courtyard of Valastro house. Toward evening.

The men lift the nets to their shoulders as they prepare to leave.

ANTONIO: Everybody ready?

COLA: Yes, let's go.

They go off, saying goodbye to the women standing in the doorway.

ANTONIO: Bless me, Mother.

MOTHER: God bless you.

COLA: Bless me, Mother.

MOTHER: God bless you.

ANTONIO: 'Bye, Lucia.

LUCIA: 'Bye, Antonio.

Maccherone, carrying the oars, is the last to leave. Lucia closes the court-yard door. The mother and Lia go back into the house as Lucia stops to watch and Mara comes forward slowly as if answering a call. A male voice is heard singing a popular Sicilian song.

VOICE: We talk... we wrote... we look at each other... in the
    crowd...

Valastro house: Women's bedroom. Toward evening.

Mara puts a kerchief on her head, then goes to the wardrobe, takes out an apron and puts it on. She looks toward the window, smiling and listening to the song. Then she fills a glass with water from the sink and opens the window.

In front of Mara's window. Toward evening.

Mara waters the basil plant on the window sill, leaning her head against the wall as she listens to the song being sung by one of the laborers working on a new building facing the Valastro house. One of the men, Nicola, comes down a ladder carrying an empty bucket.

MARA: Hello, Nicola.

NICOLA: Good evening, Mara.

Nicola comes forward, smiling and embarrassed. Mara smiles at him.

MARA: Jano's always in a good mood, isn't he? He's always singing!

Nicola laughs, looking at his companion, then turns back to Mara and sits down against the wall facing her window.

NICOLA: Jano's only a kid, he hasn't any worries.

MARA *(affectionately)*: And you're not happy, Nicola?

NICOLA *(smiling in embarrassment)*: For me to be happy, Mara... *(Taking courage, he comes up to Mara's window and leans against the wall.)* ... There're a lot of things I need first!

MARA *(smiling)*: And just what do you need, Nicola?

NICOLA: Eh! I can't tell you that!

Mara becomes serious and lowers her eyes. To overcome his embarrassment, Nicola takes some nuts out of his pocket and begins to pry them open with his penknife.

NICOLA: Tomorrow I have to go to Catania.

MARA: What for?

Nicola offers Mara an opened nut.

NICOLA: I have to go pick up some cement.

Jano's song ends. Ciccio, the boy who assists the laborers, laughs as he shovels and turns to his companions.

CICCIO: Nicola's going to Catania to look for a wife!

Mara's face falls; Nicola laughs at Ciccio's jest.

MARA: Is that true, Nicola?

Nicola becomes serious and then smiles at Mara.

NICOLA: If I were able to marry I wouldn't have to go to Catania!

Mara caresses the basil leaves.

MARA: See how big the basil's grown. I just planted it a week ago!

NICOLA: You've got a wonderful touch for everything!

JANO: Nicola! *(Nicola and Mara turn to look at Jano, who is standing on the roof of the new building.)* Are you still jabbering? Hurry up with the tiles—it's late, we have to go home!

NICOLA: Jano, pipe down, I'm coming. *(Turning to Mara)* Well, goodbye, Mara.

MARA: Goodbye, Nicola.

Nicola slowly crosses back to the new building and begins to work again. Mara closes the shutters as Nicola gazes at her once more.

From the beach. Evening.

The boats, lit up, pull off for the night's fishing. The rocks stand out darkly on the horizon. Voices in the distance, then church bells.

On the sea. Night.

The fishing boats crisscross over the dark sea amid the reflections of their lanterns.

Long calls, warnings, signals—all indistinguishable.

On the sea. Night.

On one of the boats the fishermen begin pulling in a netful of fish.

On the sea. Night.

A group of boats. The Valastros' boat is beside Bandiera's. An argument is in progress; the voices are at first indistinct, then Antonio's and Bandiera's are heard. On the Valastro boat Vanni is mending a net, while Antonio, seated in the stern and smoking a cigarette butt, turns to his brothers and to the other fishermen.

ANTONIO: There's no point in sweating so much. The sea's dry and the night's black. There are too many boats and there's nothing we can do about it. Even if the lot of you work together...the Trezza sea would have to be as big as all of Catania!

COLA: Yes? What good would that do? The fishermen of Trezza could use it for a mirror!

The grandfather is beside Cola; Vanni listens.

GRANDFATHER: This is the sea God gave us, and we have to make do with it.

Antonio tosses away his cigarette.

ANTONIO: Yes, Grandfather, God gave us this little bit of sea beyond the rocks... *(Hits the gunwales)* and He gave us these boats too... that we can't go far out in... but Grandfather, God didn't invent the dealers who are always exploiting us fishermen!

Behind the grandfather, Cola and Vanni, the oarsmen, are eating.

GRANDFATHER: Giovanni, get me the breadbasket.

The boy goes and brings back the breadbasket. Cola drinks some wine and then turns to Antonio:

COLA: I know what Grandfather means. When things don't go well there's no use blaming others for it. *(He puts down the bottle and turns to the grandfather.)* But Grandfather, you have too much faith in people. You think they're all as honest as you are.

ANTONIO: That's right; I can't stand to see this kind of dirty deal, that they get rich at our expense!

Old Peppino, rowing on Bandiera's boat, calls to the Valastros.

PEPPINO: Boys, that's what the agreement is. You talk a lot, but we're bound to give them the fish!

BANDIERA: Well, we're bound only up to a certain point! We're bound as long as you old men take care of selling the fish! They always end up taking advantage of you. Isn't that right, Antonio?

GRANDFATHER: Don't say such things, Bandiera!

BOY *(eating beside Bandiera)*: You're too good!

PEPPINO: You talk and you talk and you always get mad at us old men. Why don't you try going on the wharf yourselves instead of us? We'll see how good you are!

COLA: Uncle Peppino, don't be offended if we talk this way. You know how we young men are. We want to poke our fingers into injustice... like Saint Thomas. So if Grandfather lets us, tomorrow we want to go on the wharf ourselves!

GRANDFATHER: I never saw the likes of it, the young men taking over the old men's business. But go on if you want to, but remember they're always in the right.

BANDIERA *(to grandfather)*: See, Uncle Vanni? We just want to try. *(To the others)* What do you think?

VOICE: Boys, I'm still agreed.

OTHER VOICES: I'm agreed too!

BOY: Of course, we're all agreed on something like this!

Alfio, seated beside two oarsmen, jumps up.

ALFIO *(shouting)*: I'm agreed too!

All the men laugh at little Alfio.

From the beach. Dawn.

With their lanterns still blazing, the boats return from the night's fishing. Calls and shouts; church bells.

Beach. Morning.

Antonio is bargaining for the sale of the fish. Maccherone stands beside him in the group of fishermen and dealers.

ANTONIO: Maccherone, go see how much fish on the scales.

Maccherone obeys as Lorenzo begins to inveigh against Antonio.

LORENZO: So that's your good catch, Antonio? It's six kilos. How much will you give me?

ANTONIO: I'll give you what I want to! Five kilos.

LORENZO: Why just five?

ANTONIO: Because!

LORENZO: All right, five kilos. *(To a wholesaler)* How much will you give me?

WHOLESALER: Four hundred.

LORENZO: Four hundred...four hundred...ten lire...four hundred ten... fifteen... fifteen...

One of Cola's men whispers something in his ear. Cola moves through the crowd and stops in another group. There are indistinguishable shouts and quarreling. Raimondo, in another group of fishermen and wholesalers, whirls some fish around in the air, then throws them to the ground and continues to shout.

RAIMONDO: Seventy-five...seventy-five...eighty...eighty-five...

LORENZO: Four hundred twenty... four twenty-five... four twenty-five...four hundred twenty-five lire...four hundred twenty-five lire...

Lorenzo nods shrewdly as a colleague murmurs something in his ear. Antonio follows the broker's game with a black expression, then suddenly grabs his lapel.

ANTONIO *(shouting)*: Lorenzo, stop selling!

Lorenzo tries to hold him back but Antonio rushes furiously away, pushing his way through the crowd and making for the scales. Throwing the contents of one of the scales to the ground, he begins to shout.

ANTONIO: Boys, listen to me!

Lorenzo tries to get to him but other fishermen hold him back.

LORENZO: My scales! My scales!

Antonio runs toward the cliff, waving the scales in the air. His words are covered by the general uproar. The dealers and the fishermen begin to brawl. Even the young boys get into it, trying to help out those of the fishermen who are getting the worst of it.

ANTONIO: What are we waiting for? Look what I'm going to do with these devil's scales! I'm throwing them into the sea!

Antonio throws the scales from the cliff into the sea just as Lorenzo reaches him. They begin to fight as other fishermen and dealers join battle too. The villagers hear the goings-on and rush down to the beach. One of the struggling men tries to escape by jumping into the water and swimming toward the beach; his opponent immediately follows suit. A fisherman grabs another set of scales and throws it into the sea as some of the dealers try to stop him.

Street in front of the Treasury Guards headquarters. Morning.

Don Salvatore is leaning against the railing. Nino runs up to the building.

NINO: Sergeant!

DON SALVATORE: What's the matter?

Nino goes up onto the balcony, where several guards are playing checkers.

NINO *(still shouting)*: Hurry! On the wharf! They're throwing the fish into the sea! Hurry up!

Don Salvatore turning to the guards, tries to reassure him.

DON SALVATORE: Hurry up, hurry up.

NINO: Hurry, sergeant! They've thrown in the fish and the scales! Hurry!

The guards take their pistols and run out with Nino and Don Salvatore.

Beach. Morning.

The guards race onto the beach as almost everyone else runs away. Those who continue to fight are separated by the guards and taken away. The shouting gradually quiets down.

Raimondo's house: Dining room. Day.

Raimondo is eating dinner; Nino and Pandolla, two wholesalers, sit near him. Lorenzo is leaning against the door. A woman brings in the food as Raimondo, wiping his sweating face, turns to the others.

RAIMONDO: Boys, we've got to try to fix up this mess. We can't go on this way. Since Antonio was arrested no one in town's working much except the good-for-nothings. Our best men are gone, the ones they arrested with Antonio. Since that business the whole town's full of communism.

LORENZO: You're right there, Raimondo!

RAIMONDO: And that's not good for us either. We can't work like this; we have to forgive Antonio!

LORENZO: I agree with you. What do you say, Pandolla?

Pandolla answers by shaking his head, not very convinced.

NINO: No, Raimondo, we've got to punish him whatever it costs, that damned bastard Antonio! Even if we never work again!

RAIMONDO: Calm down, Nino. You're right but I'm older and

I have more good sense than all of you. What good's Antonio to us in prison? But when he's out we'll send him fishing and we'll profit by it, understand?

PANDOLLA: But Antonio deserves a good lesson!

Lorenzo comes over to the table as Raimondo watches him.

LORENZO: That's enough; Raimondo's the oldest and we've got to listen to what he says.

Raimondo hands him a letter.

RAIMONDO: Right, Lorenzo. You take the co-op truck and go to Catania, give this letter to the police and tell them we're withdrawing our complaint and to let him out as soon as possible, so you can bring him right back with you.

Lorenzo starts out.

LORENZO: All right, I'll get the truck and go to Catania right now. *(He stops at the door and turns around.)* Can I take Michele Pichera with me?

RAIMONDO: Take him!

LORENZO: All right.

NINO: Raimondo, I don't agree!

Pandolla rises and comes over to the table.

RAIMONDO: Calm down. I know you're right. But if we don't we'll never get back to business!

PANDOLLA: Raimondo's always right!

He winks and gives Nino a loud raspberry. Raimondo breaks out laughing.

Valastro house. Women's bedroom. Day.

As she makes up her bed, Lucia is telling a fairy tale to Lia, who is sitting on a stool smiling.

LUCIA: And the king's son, as handsome as the sun, rides on a beautiful white horse for a year, a month, and a day, until he gets to an enchanted fountain, full of milk and honey. He gets down from the horse to drink, and what does he find? *(She smiles and gestures.)* My ring! The fairies brought it there! And when the king's son sees my ring...*(She sits down on the bed)* he falls in love with me! He rides... *(Lucia, leaning against the bedstead, has a spellbound, faraway look in her eyes as she tells the story.)* ... and rides... and rides... until at last he gets...*(Smiling and watching her sister)* to Trezza! To find me...to marry me! *(Lia listens with a serious expression.)* And he takes me, he puts me on his beautiful white horse...*(With a faraway look and a sigh, Lucia ends the story.)*...and he takes me far, far, far away... with him!

Someone knocks at the window.

VOICE OF DON SALVATORE: May I?

Lucia, startled, looks toward the window, where Don Salvatore salutes military style and speaks gallantly to her.

DON SALVATORE: Miss Lucia, please forgive me if I've taken this liberty... *(Lucia gets up, listening to Don Salvatore with eyes lowered.)* But I've been told that Antonio... *(As she hears her brother's name, Lucia suddenly smiles and comes toward the window, leaning against the headboard of the bed, which stands directly under it)* has been released by the Catania police... and I wanted to be the first to bring you the good news!

Lucia smiles with joy. On the stool behind her, Lia watches and laughs.

LUCIA: Then he'll be home right away?

DON SALVATORE *(patronizing)*: Yes, right away, right away. That makes you happy now, eh?

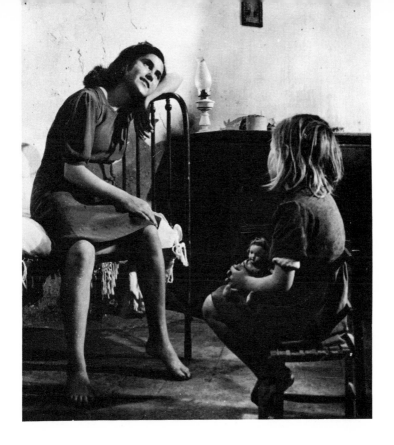

Lucia runs to the door.

LUCIA: I'll run and tell my mother! *(She stops at the door, turns to him again and lowers her eyes.)* Goodbye, Don Salvatore. And thanks!

DON SALVATORE *(saluting)*: You're quite welcome, Miss Lucia: my duty!

Lucia, smiling, closes the door behind her. Don Salvatore has stopped smiling. He looks inside the room, then again toward the door through which the girl has disappeared, then goes off whistling.

Village square. Day.

The truck bringing back the arrested men drives up and stops in the square near the sea. The people crowd around it, joyfully calling and greeting the men. Among the first to get down from the truck are Cola and Antonio. The men go off, followed by the crowd. Lorenzo and Michele remain beside the truck.

LORENZO: Let's go, Michele, come on.

Courtyard of Valastro house. Day.

Lucia is peeling potatoes in front of the kitchen door. Inside the kitchen, the mother is standing at the stove. She picks up a pot and takes it into the dining room. Vanni is sitting in the doorway singing.

Valastro house. Dining room. Day.

Cola, Antonio, and the grandfather are seated at the table. Mara is sewing. The mother enters with the pot, which she places on the table. As Cola slices the bread, the mother fills the plates with soup. Vanni's song is heard in the distance. Antonio is about to start eating but then pushes his plate away.

ANTONIO: I don't want any.

MOTHER: Why not, Antonio?

ANTONIO: I don't want any.

He gets up from the table.

MOTHER: Antonio, eat.

ANTONIO: I don't want any.

GRANDFATHER: What do you get by not eating, Antonio?

Antonio lights a cigarette before answering.

ANTONIO: Grandfather, that's not the point, eating or not. It's something else.

Cola and Mara turn to him.

GRANDFATHER: Well, what is the point, Antonio?

Antonio turns back to the table suddenly and speaks to the entire family.

ANTONIO: Did you see? They put us in jail because the law says we committed a crime. But when it suits their purpose the law doesn't count any more. So they spring us! Can you understand what this means? I'll tell you!

Antonio takes a chair near the door through which Lucia now enters, stopping to listen. Antonio sits down at the table and continues to talk, growing increasingly excited.

ANTONIO: It means they need us!

COLA *(bitterly)*: How can anyone need us? We're just draft animals, like Jano's donkey. Who could need us? The fish, to get themselves caught!

ANTONIO *(excited)*: I tell you they need us! So why do we always have to be under them! Let's forget them! And see how they do then! Let's see how far they get without us!

GRANDFATHER: Antonio, whoever leaves the old road finds a worse road!

ANTONIO: Grandfather, your proverbs were good once upon a time but not any more! Don't think I've gone crazy. I think with my head, not my feet! I don't want to hurt anybody. *(He hits the table.)* But I tell you we weren't born to be beggars, to not even hope to better our lives ... but to at least control our own lives and those of our families!

GRANDFATHER: Your father always worked and he never complained!

COLA: Yes, but our father drowned, past Cape Mulini. Who ever thanked him? After he slaved all his life for other people! Who ever thinks of him now, or of all the other men who've died at sea slaving for other people? *(He hits the table and suddenly stands up and goes over to the window.)* Antonio's right! I'm not sure why, but Antonio's right! *(He leans against the wall and speaks to the whole family.)* If we worked on our own, everything we did would be for our house, for our mother and our sisters. When our father was alive he understood these things. He'd have gone along with Antonio. He sure wouldn't have wanted his sons to keep on like this!

Antonio hits his hand against the table and stands up, shouting.

ANTONIO: You see, you understand too.

Vanni, off-screen, stops singing. Lucia comes to the table as Antonio walks toward the door.

ANTONIO: If we all agree, we'll be rid of these bloodsuckers forever!

COLA: What should we do, Antonio?

ANTONIO: I want to get free of these "dealer" crooks and free you all too! *(He turns around to face the family as the mother silently carries the pot back to the kitchen.)* We'll work on our own, with our own boat! *(Vanni enters from the courtyard to listen and leans against the doorway.)* And our women'll help salt the fish... *(Cola comes over to his brother.)* And we'll sell it and go right to Catania!

COLA: It'll take money to do that, and we haven't got any!

ANTONIO: Don't worry, Cola; we have the house!

Antonio puts his hand on Cola's shoulder and goes out into the courtyard with him. Lucia, the grandfather, and Vanni watch them go.

Courtyard of the Valastro house. Day.

Cola and Antonio come out of the house into the courtyard.

COLA: What d'you mean, we have the house? You want to sell it?

Antonio sits down under the tree; Cola follows him.

ANTONIO: Not sell it, mortgage it: that's how we'll get the money! When we get the money we'll work for ourselves and little by little we'll pay off the debt.

COLA: If the others agree, I agree too. *(Antonio, delighted to have been understood, slaps Cola's knee.)* The point is, if everybody agrees. *(At the kitchen door, the mother picks up the chair left by Lucia and brings it into the house.)* And our mother has to consent.

Vanni, in the doorway, smiles as he turns to watch his mother coming in. Lucia comes forward, laughing and listening with interest.

Village tavern. Outside. Day.

Groups of loungers, peddlers, and little boys are chatting and arguing before the entrance to the tavern. Antonio approaches, stops a moment beside one group, then enters the tavern with another fisherman.

Tavern. Inside. Day.

Antonio enters the crowded tavern and jokingly greets Bandiera, who is playing cards with some other fishermen at one of the tables.

ANTONIO: Cards as usual, eh, Bandiera?

BANDIERA: What do you expect, Antonio? I'm playing for a glass of wine!

Antonio continues on toward the wine counter.

NAPOLI: You didn't see any wine in the clink, Bandiera!

Everyone laughs. The fisherman who entered with Antonio turns to Bandiera's opponent.

FISHERMAN: What're you taking him on for? He'll beat you! What're you playing with him for?

PLAYER: If I don't get some good cards...

FISHERMAN: Even if you do...

Antonio comes back to Bandiera's table to drink his wine. Lorenzo, the fish dealer, enters and goes to the counter. Napoli consoles Bandiera's opponent.

NAPOLI: He's sharp... he's sharp...

Antonio turns to Bandiera, winking.

ANTONIO: Bandiera, here's our "friend."

Lorenzo overhears, although Antonio has not spoken loudly. Antonio and Napoli turn toward Lorenzo with an almost aggressive air.

NAPOLI: Greetings, Lorenzo!

All laugh. Bandiera throws down a card.

BANDIERA *(exclaiming half-seriously)*: He really is our friend! If it weren't for him we'd still all be in jail!

He gestures to express manacled hands. The fisherman who came in with Antonio crosses over to Lorenzo and laughs, as Antonio speaks to the others.

ANTONIO: Boys, I've got an idea. *(Lorenzo, smoking, comes toward the group; at Bandiera's table the card game stops.)* But I'm afraid our friend won't like what I have to say!

Lorenzo glares menacingly at them all.

LORENZO: Remember, boys, I'm everybody's friend and nobody's, but don't anybody try to cross me!

He looks at them one by one and then starts to go out. After a moment's silence, Napoli sends a loud raspberry after him. The others all follow his example. Lorenzo turns indignantly. All the men assume an air of false indifference. Antonio whistles innocently. Everyone laughs.

A FISHERMAN: Is there a concert today?

Laughing, he comes up to Lorenzo; Lorenzo goes out. The laughter increases.

The Co-operative. Outside. Day.

Nino, seated before the entrance, listens to Lorenzo, who has just arrived. Two old men are sitting on the ground; another stands next to the door. A boy passes back and forth.

LORENZO: It's useless! These "friends" just never change! They'd rather be worse off than better!

NINO *(standing up)*: Don't worry about it, Lorenzo. We'll bring them back in line little by little, you'll see. Right, Raimondo?

Raimondo comes out of the building, laughing.

RAIMONDO: The worm says to the rock: give me time and I'll drill a hole right through you!

Raimondo accompanies his words with an expressive gesture. He and Nino laugh.

LORENZO *(to Raimondo)*: Look, look; they're leaving!

NINO: Where're they going?

RAIMONDO: Where do you think? To the beach, to get some fresh air!

NINO: They're awfully drunk.

Another dealer comes up to Nino. They all look toward the harbor. The group of fishermen, Antonio among them, crosses the street. Some turn to look at the co-op, then they all go down the steps leading to the beach.

LORENZO: I'm surprised at Antonio, after all we've done for him!

NINO: Don't worry, you'll see, little by little...

Raimondo's laugh covers the comments of the other dealers.

Beach. Day.

Led by Antonio, the fishermen cross the beach, where other men are mending nets near the boats. Antonio runs over to one of the boats and sits down on the prow. The others gather around him to listen.

ANTONIO: Listen to me, boys, I'll tell you what I'm thinking of doing. We've had our eyes shut tight for so long, maybe for centuries...even our fathers and our grandfathers too... and we can't even see things clearly any more. You all saw what happened a few days ago. Why should you go on letting Raimondo, Lorenzo, and the rest of them ruin you? Do they risk anything? They get all the profit and none of the risk. We're the ones who risk everything; we risk the boats and our equipment, and our little brothers risk ending up just like us, locked up in the same cage of poverty! I know you're always thinking these things too. I've done it myself so many times. I know how you get to a certain point and everything gets confused in your heads, like in the baskets when the fish swim around and around and can't find a way out. So then we resign ourselves. But we've got to stop this thing at all costs! Of course they'll threaten us! They'll try to scare us! But we mustn't be scared of them! If a few of us start to work

for ourselves, the others'll take courage and follow us!
And then they'll thank us!

He smiles as he finishes, enthusiastic about his project.

Valastro house. Dining room. Day.

*The Valastro family is preparing to leave for Catania. Everyone is busy
except for the grandfather, who holds the crying baby on his lap. Lucia is
combing her hair before the mirror. The mother is combing Lia, who kneels
on a chair.*

ANTONIO: Lucia, bring me a clean pair of socks!

LUCIA: Right away, Antonio!

VANNI: Where's my tie?

MOTHER: There, on the sideboard.

Cola comes out of the men's bedroom.

COLA: Are these my socks?

LUCIA: No, they're Antonio's. Yours are on the table.

She goes into the next room.

COLA: Ah, you're right.

Mara comes over to put on the baby's bonnet.

MARA: You're all ready, Lia. Stay here and don't move.

VANNI: Mara, tie my tie.

COLA: Mine too.

*Alfio is sitting on the table; the mother goes to comb his hair. Mara knots
Vanni's tie as Cola comes over and waits his turn.*

COLA: Mine too!

Alfio runs to take a loaf of bread.

ALFIO *(turning to his mother)*: I'm taking a little bread.

ANTONIO: Everybody ready? The bus leaves in fifteen minutes.

Mara knots Cola's tie.

MARA: We're ready, Antonio! I'm just finishing Cola's tie.

She closes one of the drawers of the sideboard as Cola goes to comb his hair in front of the mirror.

MOTHER: Mara, get me my shawl on the dresser.

MARA: Here's your shawl, Mother.

She drapes the shawl over her mother's shoulders, then helps Alfio into his jacket.

MARA: Alfio, come here. Put on your jacket.

The baby continues to cry on the grandfather's lap. The mother, holding Lia by the hand, goes toward the door. Cola is sitting on the edge of the table; he shouts to his mother.

COLA: Mother, make her shut up, she's driving me crazy!

MARA: She sees all these goings-on, that's why she's crying.

Antonio comes out of the bedroom and goes to look at himself in the mirror.

ANTONIO: Hurry up, hurry up, let's go, it's late and we'll miss the bus. We have to be in Via Ospedaliera by eleven.

MOTHER: Lucia, give me the baby.

Lucia puts the baby in the mother's arms.

VOICE OF "BLONDIE": Antonio, hurry up, the bus is coming.

ANTONIO: Here we come, Blondie.

He puts an arm around the mother's shoulders and starts out the door.

BLONDIE *(at the door)*: Otherwise you'll have to wait another half-hour!

Lucia closes the shutters before leaving.

ANTONIO: Grandfather, let's go!

VANNI: Grandfather! *(Laughing)* Grandfather's bewitched, Antonio!

The grandfather seems to be in a state of shock: he is still sitting at the table and is staring into space.

ANTONIO: Let's go, Grandfather! *(Coming back to the old man)* Come on, we have to go!

BLONDIE: Start walking, start walking, I'll walk you to the bus stop.

The grandfather gets up with his grandchildren's help. Mara puts the loaf of bread in the table drawer.

MARA: Cola, let's go!

LUCIA: Alfio, Alfio, come here!

She takes the boy's hand and starts out.

Courtyard of Valastro house. Day.

Lucia comes running out of the house holding Alfio's hand; Cola follows and finally Mara, who locks the door.

ANTONIO: Mara, let's go!

MARA: I'm coming, soon as I lock the door!

She runs off after the others.

Street. Day.

Led by Blondie, the Valastro family crosses the street. A young man leans against the wall playing an accordion. Some laborers are working on the balcony of a nearby house.

ANTONIO: Hurry up, hurry up!

BLONDIE: Come on, we're almost there! Hurry!

Out on the highway the bus is approaching.

ANTONIO: Hurry, hurry!

The bus pulls up and stops; the Valastros run to get on, Blondie helping them and closing the door after them.

BLONDIE: Have a good trip! Goodbye!

The bus drives off and Blondie starts back into town.

Street. Day.

Antonio comes walking up the street, greeting the women as he passes.

A NEIGHBOR: Here's Antonio!

ANOTHER NEIGHBOR: Are you back, Antonio?

ANTONIO: I'm back, I'm back! Hello, everybody!

NEIGHBORS: Hello, hello!

Antonio enters the courtyard of his own house, where two bands nailed to the rotting door read: "For Our Beloved Father" and "For My Dear Husband." As he crosses the courtyard he greets his grandfather.

ANTONIO: Bless me, Grandfather!

Valastro house. Dining room. Day.

The mother is working near the door. Vanni enters, radiant.

VANNI: Mother, Antonio's back! Mara, Antonio's back!

Antonio enters the house and greets his mother.

MOTHER: Antonio, you're back? God be praised!

ANTONIO: Yes, Mother, I'm back! Good news! I've been to the bank! There were so many people there, it seemed like they were crazy! But I kept my head! They gave me the money and now we'll get everything set!

Valastro house. Men's bedroom. Day.

Antonio opens the door and enters the bedroom, where Cola is shaving.

COLA: You're back, Antonio?

ANTONIO: Yes, I'm back, Cola. Everything's set now so we can buy everything we need.

COLA: Didn't you put the money in the bank?

Antonio shows his brother the bank book before putting it in the dresser drawer.

ANTONIO: Here's the book! Now we won't have to work for other people any more! We'll work for ourselves, and we'll bring home all the money we make! *(He takes off his jacket.)* Little by little we'll pay off our debt and some day I'll want to get married!

COLA: You want to get married, Antonio?

ANTONIO: Yes, I want to get married, Cola! And what about you, don't you have your eye on some girl?

COLA: No, I don't have my eye on any girl!

ANTONIO: I do. I do have my eye on a girl!

His hands in his pockets, Antonio smiles as he leans against the back door. Giovannina, hanging up the laundry outside, sees Antonio and greets him.

GIOVANNINA: Antonio, back from Catania?

ANTONIO: Yes, I'm back from Catania.

GIOVANNINA: Now are we supposed to call you "Boss Antonio"?

Antonio goes out toward her as Cola, still shaving, watches him.

ANTONIO: With God's help and our work, we'll make it! *(Singing)* My treacherous looove, my loove... You didn't become a hoooly nun... I weep, I weep, I die... I die...

Vegetable garden. Day.

Still singing, Antonio leans against a tree, looking into Giovannina's eyes; she has stopped work to listen to him.

ANTONIO *(singing)*: Without you...I die without yooou!

GIOVANNINA: A happy man sings! Good for you!

ANTONIO: Yes I'm happy, for I won't kill myself any more working for other people, I'll work for myself now!

Blondie greets Antonio from the terrace of a nearby house.

BLONDIE: Antonio! The world's made of stairs; some go up and some go down!

ANTONIO: Pfuuuh!

BLONDIE: You spitting at me, you louse?

Antonio goes toward the terrace.

ANTONIO: Yes, for you just say that to hurt me!

BLONDIE: You're a fool! *(To another neighbor)* Look how stuck-up he is now!

VICENZA *(from another terrace)*: Antonio! Neighbors are like roof tiles! They're always pouring water on each other!

He laughs. Antonio sits down on the ground.

ANTONIO: If things turn out well for me, I'll remember my friends! *(Nunzio is playing "My Treacherous Love" on a pipe, from the window of his house.)* Uncle Nunzio, you're ribbing me too?

Antonio laughs happily and stretches out on the ground with his legs crossed. The sound of the pipe continues.

GIOVANNINA: Maria! Look at Antonio! He just sings and laughs and insults everybody.

VOICE: He's so stuck-up now!

She laughs. The neighbors all laugh; Antonio, happy, joins them.

On the sea. Evening.

On the Valastro boat, Antonio is rowing energetically; his face is radiant. Cola and Maccherone can be seen behind him.

ANTONIO: Look where you're going! Farther over on this side! Farther over! *(He stops rowing.)* Boys, let's put up the sail, there's a little wind now! Francesco, come help me with the sail!

FRANCESCO *(coming over to Antonio)*: Yes.

With Francesco's help, Antonio raises the sail. Background music begins, slow and solemn. The Valastro boat, in the middle of the little fleet, glides out to sea past the rocks. The music fades.

Beach. Night.

The boats return to shore after the night's fishing. An old man shouts from the beach.

OLD MAN: Antonio!

VOICE FROM BOATS: Oh!

OLD MAN: What've you caught?

VOICE: A whole lot of anchovies!

OLD MAN: Where'd you get them?

VOICE: Way out! Way far out!

OLD MAN: How deep?

VOICE: Forty!

OLD MAN: Did the other boats get any?

VOICE: One of your boats got some!

OLD MAN: Where were you? Far out?

VOICE: At forty, we were, at forty!

The Valastro boat has drawn nearer: the grandfather and Cola pull in their oars. The men lift up the nets full of shining anchovies and begin to unload them into the baskets.

COLA: Giovanni, don't let them drop on the deck. It's been so long since we've got any of these... a whole year! Better you should throw them back in the sea!

Salt shop. Inside. Day.

The shop boy throws a sack of salt on the scales.

SHOP BOY: That's five sacks, Uncle Turi.

TURI: Thirty kilos...two hundred seventy and thirty... *(After weighing the salt, Turi goes over to the counter at the entrance, where Mara follows his reckoning attentively.)* ...makes exactly three hundred kilos; at ten lire a kilo that makes three thousand lire. All right?

Mara glances outside, makes a rapid calculation on her fingers, and then gives her answer.

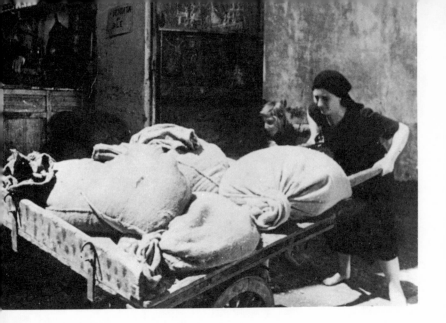

MARA: Right, Uncle Turi.

She takes the money from her blouse.

Outside the salt shop. Day.

Mara pays Turi as the shop boy takes the last sack outside. She counts the thousand-lire bills out carefully.

MARA: One...two...and three.

Turi finishes filling another sack on the counter.

TURI: And here's the fifty kilos of coarse salt for pickling.

MARA: All right, Uncle Turi; put it on the wheelbarrow.

TURI: Right away.

Mara leaves as the shop boy returns. Lia is standing beside the wheelbarrow, which is heaped with sacks of salt.

MARA: Let's go, let's go, Lia. *(She starts to push the wheelbarrow but it is too heavy for her; she looks around and shouts.)* Hey, kids! Can you help me push the wheelbarrow? It's too heavy for me!

Six or seven youngsters run toward Mara from the beach. Turi places the last sack on the wheelbarrow.

TURI: Good luck, Mara, and good salting!

Laughing and enthusiastic, the little boys push the wheelbarrow up the sun-drenched street. A smaller boy runs after the group as a passer-by greets Mara.

Street. Day.

The boys push Mara's wheelbarrow up a little street where some laborers are working. Some workmen are coming down a nearby alley. The first of them goes off whistling. Among them is Nicola, who carries a sack of cement on his shoulders. He puts down the sack and runs to help Mara push the wheelbarrow up the alley. They stop. The little boys continue to fool around and laugh near the wheelbarrow.

A WOMAN: What've you bought, Mara, salt?

Mara takes the kerchief from her head and sits down for a moment to catch her breath. Nicola stands facing her.

MARA: Thanks, Nicola, thanks! A good thing you were there! I couldn't go another step!

Lia comes to stand beside her sister. Nicola smiles. Mara fans herself with her kerchief.

MARA: Ah! It's so hot!

NICOLA: Rest a little while, Mara.

She fastens her hair behind her neck.

MARA: I can't stop; they're waiting for the salt at home! *(She continues to speak with a hairpin between her teeth.)* You know, Nicola, this is the fifth load I've brought this morning!

NICOLA *(obviously embarrassed)*: When do you start salting?

MARA: One of these evenings, because Antonio's caught so many anchovies! So we have to hurry up and salt them!

Nicola has lit a cigarette butt.

NICOLA: Of course you have to hurry up, otherwise they'll go bad!

MARA: Well, if we have good luck, Nicola, and they're salted well, we'll pay off the bank pretty soon. *(She rises and comes over to Nicola.)* For that debt feels like it's stuck here in our throats! *(Nicola and Mara gaze at each other; after a pause, Mara goes on.)* Well, Nicola, will you help me push the wheelbarrow the rest of the way home?

NICOLA: Of course, Mara, it's a pleasure!

He tosses away his cigarette as Mara turns to the little boys crowded around her.

MARA: All right, kids, you can go now because he'll help me! Come here, take this! Buy whatever you like!

She takes some small change from her blouse and distributes it to the children, who run off shouting. Then she takes Lia's hand as Nicola pushes the wheelbarrow.

MARA: We're all working at home now. We weave and we make nets.

NICOLA: Now your family's in business for itself, Mara, and you're going to be rich. Soon they'll find a husband for you.

MARA: God will take care of that. You know what, Nicola? I don't think about getting married.

NICOLA: How wonderful it is when a person's rich and can marry whoever they want to and can go live wherever they want to!

They stop. Mara lowers her eyes, then looks toward her house. A child is heard crying.

MARA: Here we are. You can go too; the men are waiting for you. Thank you, Nicola. *(She takes a few steps, then smiles, embarrassed.)* My brothers must be up by now. They'll help me carry in the sacks.

Nicola comes up to her.

NICOLA: Then goodbye, Mara, and I wish you good luck with all my heart: with all my heart, Mara.

He goes off down the alley and picks up his sack of cement at the corner. Mara stops to watch him, then goes toward her house calling her brothers. Some neighbors turn to watch her from the doorways of their homes.

MARA: Vanni! Alfio! Help me; here's the salt!

NEIGHBOR: You've bought the salt, eh? To salt them well!

MARA: This is the fifth load this morning!

Vanni and Alfio run out.

VANNI: We'll help you now, Mara. You bought the salt?

They load the sacks on their shoulders.

MARA: Yes, hurry. *(She helps Alfio adjust the sack on his shoulders.)* Here, take this one. Hurry up!

On the hillside. Day.

Antonio and Nedda are sitting on the hillside overlooking the sea. Her head rests on her hand; he sits close behind her, smiling. A train is heard in the distance.

ANTONIO: Well, have you made up your mind, Nedda?

NEDDA: I don't know yet.

VOICE OF NEDDA'S MOTHER: Neddaaa! *(Nedda raises her head.)* What are you up to?

Nedda gets up and shouts back.

NEDDA: I'm coming, Mother! *(Turning to Antonio)* Let's go, Antonio!

He rises too and follows the girl down the hill toward her house.

ANTONIO: Well, have you made up your mind, Nedda? Yes or no? Sunday morning I'll come get you... *(The church bells ring out joyfully and continue throughout the scene.)* ...and we'll go to Cannizzaro. We'll have a nice walk.

NEDDA: I still don't know.

ANTONIO: Come on, Nedda, let's...we'll have a good time for the whole day long.

He puts his arm around her waist. She answers, laughing.

NEDDA: I still don't know...

The couple walks on down toward Nedda's house, against the background of the sea.

Courtyard of Valastro house. Night.

Cola carries a barrel of anchovies into the courtyard as the grandfather, sitting among the other old people of the neighborhood, keeps track on a sheet of paper.

COLA: Here's another one, Grandfather.

GRANDFATHER: That makes twenty-five. It's money for this winter!

AN OLD MAN: You've got a lot there!

ANOTHER OLD MAN: Of course they do!

A WOMAN: How much did you catch?

Nunzio begins to play "Ah, non credea mirarti" from Bellini's "Sonnambula." The sound of his pipe continues throughout the scene. Cola goes out. The courtyard is full of people working at or watching the salting of the anchovies. The courtyard is illuminated by several light bulbs. Some boys are sitting on the courtyard wall. An old woman calls to the grandfather from a window.

OLD WOMAN: Uncle Vanni, you've made a fortune this year!

Voices and laughter in the background. Vanni enters the courtyard and goes up to his grandfather.

VANNI: Uncle Nunzio's giving us a concert!

Antonio is in the center of the courtyard, among the women bending over the baskets of fish. He looks around.

ANTONIO: Let's hurry up, boys!

VANNI: We're working, we're working.

He goes out.

ANTONIO: Let's hurry up, boys, there're more coming! Work faster!

Mara and the mother are working in the background beside Bandiera and Giovannina.

GIOVANNINA: Kids, can you guess this riddle? I have something with a long long nose; winter comes and away it goes!

LITTLE GIRL: The broom handle!

Everyone laughs. Antonio moves away as Mara answers.

MARA: I know what it is: a rake!

Don Salvatore appears at the courtyard entrance.

DON SALVATORE: Hello, everybody! Keep it up, keep it up!

ANTONIO: Hello, sergeant!

CHORUS OF VOICES: Hello, sergeant!

DON SALVATORE: Hello, hello! Heavens, how much fish! Never saw a salting like this!

COLA *(ironically)* : Right, sergeant? Seems there're more anchovies than Treasury Guards!

Everyone laughs. Don Salvatore smiles maliciously.

DON SALVATORE: And the anchovies have better luck than us guards, because they're being handled by all these beautiful girls!

He looks toward Lucia. The laughter increases. Lucia is working and laughing with the other women. Antonio is behind her with a barrel in his hand; he turns.

ANTONIO: Sergeant, you shouldn't say such things. *(Don Salvatore is embarrassed.)* You know what happens? The women get certain ideas in their heads!

He laughs, looking around. Lucia smiles at her brother, then turns toward the sergeant and lowers her eyes, suddenly serious. Everyone laughs. Don Salvatore tries to overcome his embarrassment. Antonio goes off with his barrel. Lucia turns to the other women, laughing.

LUCIA: See if you can guess this one! I cut off the tail, I cut off the snout, and then a beautiful lady comes out.

CONCETTA: I can guess that one! It's a prickly pear.

Everyone laughs.

DON SALVATORE *(taking his leave)* : Well, goodbye, all! Keep up the good work!

VOICES: Goodbye. God bless you, sergeant!

Bastianello Alley. Night.

Don Salvatore leaves the courtyard still saying his adieux.

DON SALVATORE: Good night, good night.

He stops for a moment in front of Nunzio, who continues his piping unperturbed. A group of children has gathered around the musician.

DON SALVATORE: Beautiful music, eh? That's Vincenzo Bellini, isn't it? The "Swan of Catania"! Good night, Uncle Nunzio!

Still playing, Nunzio acknowledges him with a nod as Don Salvatore goes up the alley.

Near Cannizzaro. Day.

His jacket over his shoulders, Antonio is being pulled laughingly along by Nedda, who is wearing a new dress. A locomotive is heard in the distance.

Antonio and Nedda run along the country road, half-hidden by the trees. The broad horizon of the sea lies in the background. The train draws nearer. Antonio and Nedda run along arm in arm. As they reach a small escarpment, Antonio jumps down and then helps Nedda.

ANTONIO: Come on, come on, Nedda!

They kiss, then Nedda breaks away as Antonio, laughing, watches her. The sound of the train grows louder. With a challenging smile, Nedda takes off her shoes and runs off; Antonio follows. They go off through the low underbrush and prickly pears.

ANTONIO: Nedda, wait! Wait! Nedda! Neddaaa!... *(The sound of the train peaks and then begins to fade off in the distance.)* Neddaaa! Neddaaa! You're going to fall into the sea! Wait, I'll save you! Wait, Neddaaa!

The train whistles in the distance. Nedda suddenly throws herself down at the edge of the cliff. Antonio runs up and sits beside her. Panting and laughing, they gaze at each other. The roar of the sea is heard below them.

Nedda slowly begins to untie Antonio's tie. She laughs. Antonio kisses her; Nedda, still holding his tie, throws her arm around his neck.

Near Cannizzaro. Day.

Lying on his stomach, Antonio looks toward the sea. Nedda, beside him, puts her shoes on. They rise and go off slowly. The sound of the sea fades into the musical background.

Street. Day.

Antonio and Nedda walk on the sunny part of a street walled in on both sides. A dark shadow divides the road in two. In the background, snow-topped Mount Etna.

After a short crescendo, the music slowly fades.

On the wharf. Day.

The Valastro boat is ready to go out. Maccherone is loading up. The wind is whipping up the sea. The Valastros and their hired fishermen appear, carrying the nets.

FISHERMAN: It's a bad day! There's a lot of wind!

ANTONIO: What're you talking about?

The men, among them Bandiera, load the nets and other things onto the boat. A man who has been sitting nearby gets up and goes over to them.

MAN: Antonio, you going out on a day like this?

The wind covers the sound of the discussion. The boat draws away. The man, Bandiera, and Alfio remain ashore.

BANDIERA: Be careful; if there's wind in the gulf, come on back! Can you hear me, Antonio? Look out, the wind may be worse in the gulf…and fish are caught in good weather!

The sound of the wind increases.

Panorama of the village. Day.

The great rocks are silhouetted on the horizon. Boats are drawn up all over the beach. A boy is ringing the church bell.

Beach. Day.

The sea is rolling heavily and the sky is dark. The church bell continues to peal.

Cliffs. Day.

The angry sea beats against the cliffs. The bell continues to ring.

Cliffs. Day.

Panorama from the cliffs toward the horizon, past the rocks. Storm. Church bell rings.

Cliffs and entrance to Bandiera's house. Day.

The sea lashes against the cliffs. The sound of the church bell continues throughout the scene. Bundled in a shawl, Mara makes her way toward the gate and calls loudly.

MARA: Bandieraaa! Bandieraaa! Open up, it's me, Mara! Bandieraaa!

She opens the gate and enters as Bandiera comes out toward her.

BANDIERA: Mara, what is it? What's happened?

MARA: Bandiera, for the love of God, help me!

Bandiera puts his arm around her shoulders and takes her with him toward the house. They stop a moment.

BANDIERA: Take it easy, calm down, come into the house.

Bandiera's house. Day.

Bandiera and Mara enter the house. He sits the girl down on the edge of the bed and then calls his wife.

BANDIERA: Sit down here, Mara. Angelina, come here, Mara's here.

MARA: I was out on the cliff all night long waiting for them! Bandiera, somebody's got to go look for them! We're scared someone'll drown!

Bandiera's wife enters with a child in her arms and stops near the bed to listen.

BANDIERA: Holy Virgin! I told him not to go out with the sea like that! How can I go out now to look for him? You can see what a storm there is!

Mara, desperate, clutches the lapel of his jacket.

MARA: Bandiera, you have to go! I haven't got the courage to go home unless I can tell my mother someone's gone out to find them! (*Mara throws herself weeping on the bed, then continues.*) You don't know how she is, she looks like a corpse, with her eyes staring that way!

BANDIERA: Courage, Mara, courage! I'll see what I can do!

Bandiera looks outside, then walks out. His wife, rocking the baby, comes silently over to the weeping Mara. The church bell is still ringing.

Cliffs. Day.

Panorama of the raging sea beating against the cliffs. The rocks stand out darkly on the horizon.

Cliffs. Day.

Wrapped in their black shawls, whipped by the wind, the Valastro women look out toward the horizon over the crashing sea. The mother holds the baby wrapped in her shawl. Sound of stormy sea throughout the scene.

The sun is setting; the storm is almost over. The women turn and start down the cliff.

Beach. Day.

Three boys are sitting on the steps leading down to the beach; some fishermen are chatting as they lean against the railing. One of the boys sees something on the horizon.

BOY: Isn't that Bandiera's boat? It's Bandiera's boat!

The men look.

MAN: It is, it is! Quick, go tell him. Come on, let's go!

As the boy runs toward the village, the group of men goes down to the beach.

Village street. Day.

The boy runs along shouting.

BOY: Bastiano, Bastiano! Bandiera's boat's coming in with Antonio's! Come down to the beach!

He continues up the street shouting out the news; the men run toward the sea. Some women working in the sun get up from their chairs. A group of children runs past the boy in the opposite direction. Indistinguishable shouts and calls.

Another group of men starts down to the sea. Among them is the boy, who imparts the news to a fisherman coming out of a doorway; the man joins the group. The women stand in the doorways as the men go down toward the sea; the whole town has heard the news.

Beach. Day.

On the pier, a group of men is watching Antonio's boat being pulled in by Bandiera's. Antonio stands in the prow, his arms folded. The two boats enter the harbor and draw up to the beach. Calls from the beach.

The group of fish dealers watches the return of Antonio; among them is Lorenzo, standing up on a boat in drydock. They go down toward the beach.

Bandiera's boat and then Antonio's are drawn up on the beach. Groups of men and boys watch the operation. Shouts and calls. Antonio, Cola, and the grandfather push their boat up on the beach. The curious crowd around it. The grandfather and Vanni start off; Antonio remains by the boat. Several of the dealers come up to Antonio.

FISH DEALER: You're ruined by your own hand!

CONTE: See what you've done now, wise guy?

Lorenzo climbs onto Antonio's boat and shouts to him.

LORENZO: You see you're not cut out for this work, you fool!
    (He passes by Antonio, slapping him on the shoulder.) Now you'll
    have to pay for it!

He goes toward the stern as the other dealers pass by Antonio.

FISH DEALER: Listen to your elders next time!

*Cola jumps down from the devastated boat. Bandiera comes over to Antonio
and slaps him affectionately on the shoulder.*

BANDIERA: Chin up, Antonio!

Antonio takes off his cap and throws it angrily to the ground.

ANTONIO: Damn the man who learned how to fish!

BANDIERA: It's not the end of the world, Antonio!

Antonio picks up his cap. Cola comes over to him.

COLA: Come on, let's go home; Mother's waiting for us.

*The two brothers go off through the murmuring crowd, followed by the
grandfather and Vanni.*

Valastro house. Dining room. Day.

*The Valastro women await their men in the half-dark house. The mother
sits in one corner; Mara stands beside Lia; Lucia rests her head on the
table. Some neighbor women are sitting with them.*

VOICE OF BOY: Antonio's back! Antonio's back! Look, look!

Mara and Lia come forward. Lucia rises, opens the door and goes out into the courtyard, followed by Mara. The mother, accompanied by a neighbor, stops in the middle of the room.

VOICE OF BOY: Antonio's back!

Shouts and greetings in the courtyard. Jano, the laborer, begins to sing. Embracing Lucia, Antonio comes into the room; Cola and Mara follow, arm in arm. Antonio embraces his mother.

MOTHER: My son, my son, my son, my son... *(He steps aside and Cola embraces her.)* My son, my son, my son!

Cola breaks away.

COLA: Mother, don't you see we're back? Take it easy!

The mother goes to the door to embrace Vanni. Antonio throws his jacket on the table. The neighbors leave as Vanni embraces little Lia. Jano is still singing in the distance. Irritated by the sound, Antonio turns and shouts.

ANTONIO: Will you shut up! *(He goes to close the window angrily, then turns and leans against the wall.)* Leave us alone! Leave us alone! Always this bad luck for me... chained to my fate! And always working to feed other people!

COLA: Don't worry if things stay the same!

ANTONIO: But I tell you we've got to get out of this!

He goes to the mirror hanging on the wall and looks at himself. Lucia, in the doorway to the men's bedroom, stops. Antonio shouts.

ANTONIO: No!

LUCIA: Keep quiet, Antonio, Grandfather can hear you!

ANTONIO *(to Mara)*: Bring me the basin, I want to shave.

Mara fills a basin with water.

MARA: Here you are, Antonio.

She brings the basin to the table, where Lia is sitting and joking with

LA TERRA TREMA : 59

Vanni. Antonio goes to wash as Cola moves toward the entrance door.

Courtyard of Valastro house. Day.

Alfio runs toward Cola.

ALFIO: Cola, Cola, Cola!

Cola takes him in his arms. Two neighbor women listen in silence and look toward the grandfather, who is sitting near the mother.

GRANDFATHER: And now we'll pay off our debt.

Cola smiles as he holds Alfio in his arms.

COLA: Grandfather, let's go in; Mother's made our supper.

The grandfather gets up and goes into the house with the mother. Slow background music begins and continues for the rest of the scene. The neighbors start off, murmuring among themselves. Cola closes the door. After a moment, Maccherone goes to sit down where the grandfather had been seated. He bites into a piece of bread and looks around happily.

Near Nedda's house. Day.

Antonio runs toward Nedda's house. The sky is overcast.

ANTONIO: Neddaaaa, come out! Neddaaa! Nedda, it's me, Antonio! Open the door!

A door slams shut. Antonio runs into the alley between the houses. He stops a moment and looks around.

ANTONIO: Neddaaaa! *(He knocks on the door that has just been closed.)* Nedda, open up! Is somebody in the house, Nedda? Neddaaaa! *(He runs to knock on the other door.)* Nedda, open up, it's Antonio! Nedda! *(He goes back toward the rabbit hutch, shouting.)* Neeeddaaa!...Neeeddaaa! Nedda! Nedda! Nobody's home? Nedda! *(He comes back, looking around.)*

Neddaaa! Neeeddaaa! *(A dog begins to bark in front of the barn; Antonio calls more quietly as he walks on.)* Nedda...

Beach. Day.

Antonio walks along the beach, where the fishermen, talking and laughing, are mending their nets and sails. Background music begins, slow and sad.

FISHERMAN: How goes it, Antonio?

Antonio stops beside a boat where two fishermen are gathering up a net. The music ends.

ANTONIO: Any work for me and my brothers?

ANGELO: Can't you see? We've got a full crew. If it was just you... I'm sorry...

ANTONIO: It doesn't matter, Uncle Angelo.

ANGELO: I'm sorry, Antonio.

The music begins again, sad and slow. Antonio goes off along the beach. Angelo and his men watch him as the others start to work again.

The music fades. Antonio comes up to a boat on which a fisherman is hammering, surrounded by onlookers. Antonio leans against the boat.

ANTONIO: Hello, Mr. Viola!

Inside the boat, Viola turns toward him.

VIOLA: Oh, hello, Antonio! What brings you here?

The fisherman stops hammering.

ANTONIO: I came to see if there's any work for me.

VIOLA: But tell me, could you learn to be a carpenter?

ANTONIO: What d'you mean, carpenter? I'm a fisherman!

The sound of hammering resumes.

VIOLA: Then I'm really sorry, you know, but I can't help you!

ANTONIO: There's nothing for it, Mr. Viola! Goodbye!

VIOLA: So long!

The music begins again as Antonio continues along the beach. He stops beside some old fishermen intent on their work, then starts rapidly back toward the village. The music ends.

Valastro house. Women's bedroom. Day.

Mara is mending; Lucia embroiders. They hear someone whistling and look toward the window.

MARA *(worried)* : Lucia, it's Don Salvatore! Don't let him see us!

She runs to sit on the bed beneath the window, as Lucia goes to the mirror. The whistling continues.

Don Salvatore opens the half-closed shutter and looks inside.

DON SALVATORE : Hello, Miss Lucia! *(Lucia, smiling, turns and leans against the dressing table; Don Salvatore gives her a military salute.)* Do you mind if I stop here a minute?

Lucia darts a glance at her sister.

LUCIA : I would if I were alone, but since my sister's here... *(Don Salvatore is visibly annoyed.)* ... there's no harm in it, is there?

DON SALVATORE : Mara's here too? Hello, Mara, you'll have to forgive me, I didn't see you.

MARA *(softly)* : Hello, Don Salvatore. You know, there's so much

gossip in town... if they saw you talking at our window... I don't mean for myself... *(She rises and goes to put a hand on the smiling Lucia's shoulder.)* ... but for Lucia, she's so young...

DON SALVATORE: You should be pleased, Miss Lucia! They talk because you're such a pretty girl! *(Lucia smiles with pleasure at the compliment. Mara has sat down behind her and continues sewing.)* They talk because they're jealous! If you weren't pretty no one would say a word. But how come you're not thinking of getting married?

LUCIA *(laughing)*: Because it just never entered my head!

DON SALVATORE: But you shouldn't marry here in Trezza... *(He moves the basil plant and sits on the window sill.)* ...because you're made for the city, not for a little village. You're made to wear fine clothes, not those rags you have on! *(Don Salvatore takes a package from his jacket.)* Let's see if you like this little thing I've brought you! It's a fine silk kerchief: seems like it's made to order for you!

Lucia breaks in abruptly, her voice rising to a shout.

LUCIA: No, no, Don Salvatore! I can't take it, I can't take it, not even if you kill me!

DON SALVATORE *(persuasively, opening the package)*: But you can at least look at it, can't you?

MARA: Don't be offended, Don Salvatore; now that we're poor these fine things aren't for us any more!

Lucia slowly approaches the window to look at the kerchief which Don Salvatore has unfolded before her.

DON SALVATORE: I'm not offended, I don't say I'm offended, but I swear I didn't deserve that!

Lucia gazes at the kerchief, enchanted, then leans back against the wall with her arms crossed and again refuses the gift.

LUCIA *(vehemently)* : No, no, no! It's too beautiful, it's too beautiful for me!

DON SALVATORE : Eh, a lot of girls have them who aren't as pretty as you!

LUCIA : Then they're rich and we're not.

DON SALVATORE : I didn't want you to think about that, but if you don't want the kerchief... I won't feel bad. *(Refolding it)* I like you all the same... all of you: Don Salvatore is always your friend! Remember that! No matter what happens! *(Departing)* Goodbye, Miss Lucia! Goodbye, Miss Mara!

MARA : Goodbye, Don Salvatore! Thank you!

She glances at her sister, then lowers her eyes to her sewing. Lucia closes the shutters and turns to her sister.

LUCIA : Anyway... Don Salvatore really is our friend. *(She sits on the bed, speaking softly, almost to herself.)* How beautiful that kerchief was. *(Lying down)* I love silk kerchiefs ... earrings ... necklaces...

Mara interrupts her sewing, rests her face on the palm of her hand, and gazes worriedly at her sister.

Courtyard of Valastro house. Day.

Three of the dealers, among them Lorenzo, are bargaining with Antonio for the sale of the salted anchovies. Mara and Lucia watch from the window, Vanni sits by the door, Cola lights a cigarette in the entrance. The mother stands at the kitchen door with the baby in her arms and Lia beside her. The grandfather is sitting on a stool smoking his pipe. Maccherone comes up.

Antonio carries a barrel of anchovies to the two men sitting in the center of the courtyard, as Lorenzo leans against the wall with a patronizing air.

ANTONIO: Here're the anchovies! *(He sits down on a stool. Alfio, carrying a pail of water, sits beside him.)* And we have another thirty barrels, same as these!

CONTE: We can be sure the stuff's all the same quality?

ANTONIO: Yes, because it was all salted at the same time, so you can be sure it's all the same.

CONTE: Just to be sure, I want to see them for myself.

LORENZO: Of course, first let's have a look and then we can talk
about prices.

*Conte opens the barrel and throws a little water on the fish to wash off the
salt. Antonio, Alfio, and the other dealer watch in silence. Conte picks up
one of the anchovies disdainfully.*

CONTE: So this is the stuff, Antonio? You can see for yourself it's
no good. *(He turns to Lorenzo and then to the other dealer.)*
Tiny little thing, full of salt, rusty...

He passes the anchovy on to the other dealer, who examines it.

DEALER: And it's dry too, Antonio. Here, catch, Lorenzo.

*He gets up and throws the fish to Lorenzo, who catches it, opens it, tastes
it, and then tosses it disdainfully at Antonio's feet.*

LORENZO: This stuff is fit for the cats!

ANTONIO: What, are you joking? The stuff is all good! You say
it's bad so you can buy it for less. That's it, isn't it? But
don't waste your breath! You won't cheat me!

VOICE OF MICHELE: Hello, everybody!

Antonio and Alfio turn as Michele, Lorenzo's driver, enters the courtyard.

MICHELE: Lorenzo, here I am with the truck, whenever you're
ready to load.

LORENZO: You can leave with the truck! There's no point in
waiting! We're not going to buy this stuff!

Lorenzo starts off as Cola comes forward and glares at the dealers.

COLA: We're in this business too, and we can judge if the stuff's
good or not! We worked to make these thirty barrels.
You think we found them in the street? Everybody leans
against the low wall, eh? But it won't work with us!

CONTE: It's just not good business for us: everybody knows his
own business! *(Getting up to leave)* Let's go.

Cola starts to follow him but Antonio gets up too and stops his brother.

ANTONIO: Let him go, Cola! They've just come to try to squeeze
   our guts!

*But Cola breaks away and runs to the courtyard entrance, where Lorenzo,
Conte, the other dealer, and Michele have stopped. Alfio clutches Cola
to hold him back, as Maccherone watches in silence.*

COLA: God damn it, we know what your business is! You know

we need money since we lost everything at sea. That's the kind of conscience you have. You want to rob us!

LORENZO: What d'you mean, rob! How many times have we come to ask you to sell? And you didn't want to then, did you? To keep it for winter! *(Lorenzo turns to his colleagues, then back to Cola, raising his voice.)* Now if you want to sell it to us, sell it; if you don't want to, you can throw it back in the sea! *(He turns to Conte, who nods approvingly.)* Our price is eighty lire!

ANTONIO *(screaming in exasperation)* : Crooks! Thieves! Get out of our house! Get out!

The baby bursts out crying in the mother's arms.

COLA *(scornfully)* : Then we do better to throw 'em back in!

Antonio comes up beside him.

LORENZO: Do whatever you like!

DEALER: Come on, let's go.

The three dealers go off; Lorenzo turns once more with an ironical look.

Michele comes up to the brothers and puts a hand on Cola's shoulder.

MICHELE: Cola...Antonio...I'm sorry they're doing this to you. All winds are bad for a broken boat!

The baby stops crying. The church bell begins to peal festively. Cola picks up Alfio as Antonio puts the opened barrel back with the others. Lucia leans on Antonio's shoulders; Mara goes over to Vanni and the grandfather to the mother. They all stare at the barrels of anchovies in silence.

Brief crescendo of music at the end of the scene, fading almost immediately as the next scene opens.

Courtyard of Valastro house. Day.

*The Valastro family watches the barrels of anchovies being taken away.
Mara and the mother are sitting beside Vanni, Cola, Alfio, and the grandfather. Antonio leans against the wall.*

*Two men remove the stones holding down the tops of the barrels lined
up along the walls and take them away one by one.*

Beach. Day.

*Slow music begins. Sound of wind on the sea. Cola walks along the deserted
cliffs under a cloudy sky. He sits down, arms folded, and gazes at the
sea. He takes out a last cigarette and throws away the empty package.*

*The music crescendos and then fades. A few fishermen are working beside
several boats drawn up on the beach. A man in a dark raincoat and hat
strolls among the boats and stops to talk to two boys working around one
of the boats.*

SMUGGLER: Hey, boys, bad weather, eh? South wind.

SANTO: Yes, bad weather...we can't go out.

SMUGGLER *(coming closer)* : It could last a week, couldn't it?

SANTO: Anything can happen, even that! *(Jano, the other boy,
laughs.)* We've been working all along and now we'll
have a little rest!

SMUGGLER: Whoever doesn't work doesn't eat.

JANO: Of course, if you don't work you don't make any money,
and you can't smoke.

SMUGGLER: Have one of these!

*Jano wipes off his hands and takes the cigarette from the pack the smuggler
offers him.*

JANO: Thanks! Can I take one for my friend too?

SMUGGLER: Sure, go right ahead.

JANO: Here, Santo!

SANTO: Good ones they are too! American! "Lucky Strike." *(Santo walks around the boat and lights the cigarette.)* We never get to smoke this kind.

SMUGGLER: You like 'em? They're good?

SANTO: Yes, yes.

SMUGGLER: Then listen to me...

He sits down on the gunwale of the boat next to Jano. Jano walks away from the boat. Another boy comes toward Jano, who gives him a taste of the cigarette. Still another boy comes up and sits on one of the boats, calling him with curiosity.

BOY: Jano! Who's that?

JANO: He's just here, with these cigarettes...

BOY: American ones?

JANO: He's got a whole pack!

Cola is walking along the beach; he passes by the smuggler and Santo.

SANTO: Cola!

Cola turns and comes over to the boat. He still has the dead cigarette butt in his mouth. Some women are washing laundry in the background.

COLA: Hi, Santo!

SANTO: Hi!

COLA: Give us a light.

Santo hands Cola his cigarette.

SANTO: This is Cola that I was telling you about. Antonio Valastro's brother. He's out of work.

Cola gives the cigarette back to Santo after lighting his own.

SMUGGLER: Is that right, Cola? You out of work like he says?

Cola, diffident and proud, throws his cigarette on the ground and answers.

COLA: Yes, it's true. Is it any business of yours?

SMUGGLER: Yes, Cola, it is. *(He gets up and goes over to Cola.)* I can help you. Have a cigarette, Cola.

Cola accepts it in silence. They walk off, talking quietly. Santo remains leaning up against the boat. The boy who had queried Jano now turns to Santo.

BOY: Santo, who's that?

SANTO: I don't know! Seems like an American to me. You should see how many cigarettes he has.

BOY: Really!

They watch Cola and the smuggler walking away and talking.

Beach. Evening.

Sounds of sea and rain. The boats are drawn up on the beach under the pouring rain. The rocks stand out against the horizon.

Valastro house. Men's bedroom. Evening.

Sound of rain. Cola enters the room and goes over to the bed. He takes a fresh pack of Luckies from his pocket and pulls off the cellophane. He glances at the window, then puts the pack back in his pocket. He hangs up his cap.

Slow background music begins. Cola walks toward the back wall. He crouches down, opens a chest, and takes out a long strip of souvenir pictures. He places it and the other objects from the chest on the edge of the bed. Last of all he takes out a military knapsack.

The door opens abruptly. The music ends. Cola turns in surprise, leaning

back against the bed. Antonio enters slowly, pulling off his jacket. Cola stands up, knapsack in hand. Antonio sees Cola and stops. Cola lowers his eyes. Antonio hangs up his jacket.

ANTONIO: Cola, what're you looking for in my navy chest? Did you find a job? I see you're taking the knapsack.

Cola throws the knapsack on the bed.

COLA: Hell no! No work! I wouldn't know what to do with it! *(He folds up the strip of photographs and replaces it in the chest.)*

Same thing today...and now they all have the excuse of the bad weather!

ANTONIO *(taking off his cap)*: Bad weather or good weather, they're all just excuses! *(He sits on the edge of the bed and dries his feet.)* I'm going crazy because we're at the end of our rope. You know, Cola, it's been a month since we started to look for work.

Cola sits on the bed and looks at a photograph of Antonio in his navy uniform which he has taken from the chest.

ANTONIO: And we haven't been able to earn a cent! *(He looks at his brother, his eyes full of tears.)* We'll have to become criminals! They've closed all the streets and they've closed all the doors! And our family'll die of hunger, and I with them! The money we got for those barrels, what good was it? And we sweated blood to make them, we were so sure that would be the start of our fortune. What good did it do to sell them? Just to keep going a little while longer. But now we've got the devil's tail on top of us; now our hopes are finished!

He drops his head in despair. Cola, still holding the photograph of Antonio in uniform, gets up from the bed, leans against the window and looks out.

COLA: I told you we should have thrown it all back into the sea, instead of playing those crooks' game. It makes my blood boil to see this kind of injustice! *(Pause)* It's gotten dark, Antonio! *(Slow music begins: Cola goes over to the dresser.)* You know something? I'm fed up with living here.

He lights the dresser lamp and sets the photograph of Antonio in the mirror frame. Then he turns back to his brother; Antonio is holding his head in his hands.

COLA: I don't believe...that in the rest of the world the people are as bad as they are here in Trezza! And I'm fed up with living here!

At Cola's words, Antonio reacts abruptly and raises his head.

ANTONIO: Don't say that! *(rising and coming over to his brother)* Because we were born in Trezza and we have to die in Trezza! *(putting a hand on Cola's shoulder)* Even if we have to suffer for it, Cola!

COLA *(gazing at Antonio's photograph)* : You can talk that way, Antonio, because you know the world. *(Smiles)* You've been to Taranto...Bari...even to La Spezia! There's a lot of world outside this village. A man could make his fortune! I want to help you, Antonio! And I want to help the family too!

ANTONIO: Cola! The sea's salty all over the world. As soon as we're outside our rocks, the current can destroy us!

Antonio lowers his face to hide his tears and goes over to the door. The last drops of rain are seen through a window beyond the open door. The music ends. Antonio turns, his voice trembling with emotion.

ANTONIO: Cola, remember this always: we have to fight our battle here! *(He goes toward the window in the next room.)* It's stopped raining.

Cola murmurs, almost to himself.

COLA: But I still want to help you, Antonio!

Valastro house. Room adjoining men's bedroom. Evening.

Antonio opens the back door and looks out, crossing his arms and leaning against the jamb. The rain continues to drip from the drainpipe.

Valastro house. Men's bedroom. Evening.

Cola stands in front of the door Antonio has just passed through. He turns as he hears the other door opening abruptly, and sees Vanni.

VANNI: Hi, Cola.

COLA: Hi.

Vanni goes into the adjoining room and greets Antonio.

VANNI: Hello, Antonio.

Cola goes back toward the bed and begins to replace Antonio's things in the chest. Alfio comes in, jumps on the bed, and starts to undress.

ALFIO: Hi, Cola. I'm going to bed.

COLA: What d'you mean, going to bed? You're soaked through, how can you go to bed like that? Vanni!

VANNI: What d'you want, Cola?

COLA: Bring me the towel, your brother's all wet!

VANNI: Wait, I'll be right there.

Alfio finishes undressing as Cola talks to him.

COLA: Look how soaking wet you are, just look; where've you been, to get so wet?

ALFIO: At the castle.

COLA: It's freezing cold! Playing with the boys?

Alfio picks up his piece of bread from the blanket and slips into bed with Cola's help.

ALFIO: Yes.

He bites hungrily into the bread, gazing at Cola, who caresses his little brother's wet hair with a serious expression.

COLA: Look how you're all soaked. You're hungry, aren't you?

Alfio nods as he takes another bite.

ALFIO: Uh huh!

Vanni finishes drying in the next room, comes over to the bed and hands Cola the towel.

VANNI: Here's the towel, Cola. *(He takes off his jacket as Cola takes the towel.)* I was working at Cannizzaro today, Cola! Picking oranges! I got three hundred and fifty lire!

He takes the money from his pocket, smiling.

Valastro house. Room adjoining men's bedroom. Evening.

Antonio closes the back door.

VANNI'S VOICE: It was a good thing they took me!

COLA'S VOICE: What were they up to? Didn't want to let you work, did they?

VANNI'S VOICE: You're right, Cola; I think they've all agreed not to let us work! After I'd been around looking for a while, Don Michele Gentile finally took me on. He needed men!

COLA'S VOICE: Put it with the rest, Vanni, the three-fifty.

Valastro house. Men's bedroom. Evening.

Antonio enters and begins to undress.

VANNI: Three-fifty, and two hundred yesterday, four hundred set aside...

COLA: Give it here, I'll put it in the drawer.

Vanni jumps onto the bed and undresses. The grandfather comes in.

ANTONIO: Blessings, Grandfather.

COLA: Blessings, Grandfather.

VANNI: Blessings, Grandfather.

GRANDFATHER: God bless you.

COLA: Isn't it better to keep it in the drawer? That way you won't lose it. *(Antonio takes a sweater from the dresser as the grandfather sits down on his bed and begins to undress.)* Because if you carry it around you could lose it. And after you've worked a whole day it would be awful to lose your pay!

Antonio pulls on his sweater, takes his cap from the bed and hangs it on the clothes rack. Slow music begins.

Cola is still dressed. Vanni hops over to the window to hang his clothes on the handle, then climbs into the big bed. Antonio gets into bed too. The grandfather blows out the light on the dresser. Cola starts out, hiding the knapsack. He looks warily around. The music fades.

Alley. Day.

It is raining. Three men come up the steep alley. They carry umbrellas and are accompanied by a local policeman.

Street. Day.

Cola hurries down a steep alley, followed by Antonio, unobserved. In the background a child is crying and a cock crows. Cola runs to join a group of young men; Antonio stops and calls to him.

ANTONIO: Cola!

The group moves off. The deafening sound of a peddler's horn drowns out the background sounds. Antonio follows his brother at a distance. Cola and his companions enter a café at the end of the street.

A group of women has gathered around the peddler's cart; he continues to sound his horn to summon other customers.

Café. Inside. Day.

Trying to remain unseen, Antonio looks through the windowpanes into the café. Cola and the others sit down at a table at which the smuggler is already seated. He offers them cigarettes.

Bastianello Alley. Day.

The three men and the policeman cross the alley as the women in the doorways watch curiously. The group stops before the courtyard of the Valastro house. The policeman knocks on the door with his umbrella handle.

POLICEMAN: Valastro! Antonio Valastro! *(Turning to the neighbors)* Tell me, isn't anybody home?

OLD WOMAN: Sure they're there. Knock louder! They're hiding, they're hiding inside!

POLICEMAN: Valastro!

He knocks once more, then opens the door.

Valastro house: Dining room. Day.

Mara opens the door of the house as the four men cross the courtyard. Vanni watches from the bedroom door as the men enter the house. Alfio, Lia, and the baby are playing on the floor; the grandfather is sitting at the table. The mother rises.

OFFICIAL: Good day. Are you the heirs of Sebastiano Valastro? We've come for the sequestration. We're officials of the Fidani Bank. *(To one of the men)* Have you got the judgment? *(The other man hands him a sheaf of papers.)* This is the judgment handed down by the magistrate of Aci Trezza, which authorizes us to proceed. *(To the other man)* Do you want to start appraising the property? Take a good look at the bearing walls *(Looking around)* and try to make an exact calculation of the area of the house.

In front of the café. Day.

Two men stand in front of the café, chatting. It is raining outside. The peddler's horn is still heard. Antonio walks past the men, looking toward the inside, where Cola is sitting at a table with the others. Antonio starts to enter the café but stops as he hears his name called.

BOY: Antonio! *(A boy runs up to him, covering his head with his jacket against the rain.)* Antonio! Antonio! Antonio!

ANTONIO: What is it? What's the matter?

BOY: Concetta's sent me. She says those Catania people are coming with the cop.

ANTONIO: Where are they? Where are they?

BOY: They're going toward your house.

Antonio glances inside the café; then, after a moment's hesitation, he runs down the street in the rain.

Valastro house: Dining room. Day.

One of the surveyors taps on the walls with the point of his umbrella; the other measures the floor area. The family and the chief official watch the operations.

SURVEYOR: The roof's in bad shape; it's got to be repaired.

OFFICIAL: Let's take a look at the other rooms.

The men go toward the bedroom as Vanni leaves his mother's side and goes over to lean against the sideboard, watching the three children playing on the floor.

Café. Inside. Evening.

Three boys are at the bar; Cola sits with the smuggler and another boy at a nearby table.

SMUGGLER: Five orangeades!... Well, boys, have you got it straight? If the weather's good, tomorrow at four in the morning at the place I told you.

One of the boys slaps another on the shoulder.

FIRST BOY: All right. We've got it. Right, Nino? Let's go.

The boy sitting beside Cola gets up.

SECOND BOY *(to smuggler)*: All right. Can I have a cigarette?

As they all leave, the first boy slaps Cola on the shoulder.

FIRST BOY: You coming too, Cola?

COLA: After a minute.

THIRD BOY: So long!

They go out, leaving Cola and the smuggler alone.

SMUGGLER: So you don't get it yet? I'll explain.

Two men come out of the back room. A man with a billiard stick turns to one of them.

MAN: Oh, Ciccio! Want to play a round?

SECOND MAN: Yes, I'll be right there.

FIRST MAN: I'll be waiting.

The smuggler draws a chalk sketch on the table top.

SMUGGLER: This is Guarnaccia Alley and this is the highway. Here's Bastianello Alley and here's your house. You go this way down to the boat...

Valastro house. Dining room. Dawn.

An alarm clock is heard ticking loudly throughout the scene. Cola opens the door and enters the dark room. He cuts a piece of bread on the table, then goes over to the family portrait hanging on the wall.

COLA *(whispering)*: Goodbye, Mother. Goodbye, Grandfather. Goodbye, Antonio; goodbye, everybody. *(He turns around.)* I'm leaving: forgive me for what I'm going to do. But I'll be back soon and we'll all be happy again.

Courtyard of Valastro house. Dawn.

Cola leaves the house, crosses the courtyard, and goes out into the alley. A cock crows sporadically.

Alley. Dawn.

Cola hurries furtively down the alley toward the sea. Cock's crow. Church bells ringing.

Cliffs. Dawn.

Cola comes up to the group waiting for him.

COLA: Anybody got a butt?

SMUGGLER: Everybody here, boys? Let's go!

A long whistle. All turn and start toward the boat. Cola is the last to climb over the gunwales. Slow sad music begins. Cola sits between two boys, his head lowered. The music crescendos over the splash of the waves, then fades slowly.

Valastro house. Men's bedroom. Day.

The grandfather sits up in bed and looks toward the boys' bed. Antonio enters and crosses the room.

ANTONIO: Cola's gone!

The grandfather falls back onto the bed.

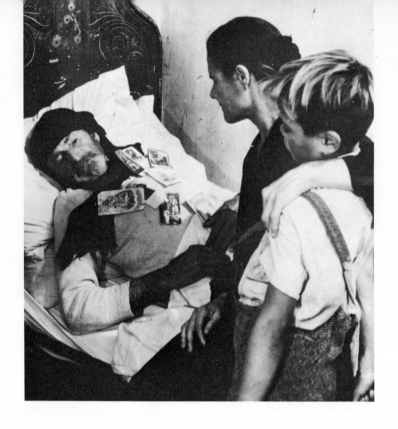

GRANDFATHER: Cola... Cola...

Valastro house. Men's bedroom. Day.

The grandfather is stretched out on the bed, with holy images laid on his chest. Beside the bed are the mother and Alfio, and an old woman whose face is buried in her hands. Antonio comes up to the grandfather's bed.

ANTONIO: The truck's here.

The mother and Alfio come forward and stop at the door, where several black-mantled neighbor women are murmuring among themselves.

VOICES: They're taking him away. ... Poor thing... They're taking
   him to Saint Martha's...

One of the old women hobbles out with the help of a cane.

In front of the house. Day.

The old woman shouts out the news.

OLD WOMAN: They're taking him away... They're taking him
   away... They're taking him away...

The old women continue their mumbled commentary.

Valastro house. Men's bedroom. Day.

Antonio picks up the old man and goes off with Mara following. The mother straightens the bed.

Courtyard of Valastro house. Day.

Mara puts a blanket over the grandfather as Antonio carries him across the courtyard and out the entrance. Mara and several neighbors follow. Lucia runs along the alley to the courtyard door and watches the group pass outside.

LUCIA *(whispering)* : Grandfather... Grandfather...

She goes toward the center of the courtyard, turns to watch some neighbors leaving, and then hides behind the wall of the house to look at an object in her hand: a glass necklace. Her face bathed in tears, she puts the necklace on and smiles.

Street. Night.

Some drunks are stretched out on the steeply rising street, Antonio among them. One man plays a harmonica; another stumbles around in a sort of dance. Antonio rises laughing and puts his hand on the dancer's shoulder; the two men laugh and stumble off up the street, holding each other up.

Antonio turns and warns the others.

ANTONIO: Shh!... Shh!...

The harmonica music stops abruptly. The drunks suddenly hush and run to hide along the wall.

The sergeant is heard whistling. He crosses the road as Antonio and his friend crouch along the wall. When he is out of sight, Antonio and then the other men emerge from their hiding places. They look around warily; a few burst out laughing. One man, carrying his shoes, goes to the corner to spy as the sergeant whistles in the distance. The others, holding their shoes, crawl over to him. The church bell rings two o'clock.

One of the drunks slaps Antonio's shoulder.

DRUNK: If the sergeant's going home at this hour he must have been arresting somebody! *(Everyone but Antonio starts to laugh; the drunk elbows the harmonica player.)* Give us some more, the sergeant's gone away!

Still holding his shoes, the musician begins to play again, as the others dance around clumsily. Antonio stares at the point where the sergeant has disappeared.

Valastro house. Dining room. Night.

Mara opens the door for Lucia, who comes in and sits at the table. Mara goes to get the lamp, lights it, and places it on the table beside her sister.

The drunk's harmonica is heard in the distance.

MARA: Where've you been?

LUCIA: Shh! Antonio'll hear you!

MARA: He's not here. He hasn't come home yet. *(Sadly)* From now on, he'll be staying out every night, and I'm here to wait for him.

LUCIA: You've been waiting for me too?

After a pause, Mara answers, looking straight at her sister.

MARA: If our mother knew, she'd die of pain... *(Lucia avoids her sister's eyes.)* ...for all the awful things that've happened!

LUCIA: What have I done? I haven't done anything wrong! So there's no harm if our mother does know! Tell her! I do what I want to, and nobody'd better say anything to me! *(Mara turns her back to her sister and hides her face in her hands.)* What do I care? Always locked up in the house like some treasure! *(She gets up shouting and crosses the room.)* Some treasure! Nobody'd marry us! You know that!

MARA *(heartstruck)*: Don't talk like that, Lucia! Now that we're poor the only thing we have is our honor! *(She crosses the room slowly and sinks onto a chair.)* We have to work, too, to help Antonio!

Lucia approaches her, shouting.

LUCIA: It was Antonio who ruined us! Now that we're so poor what does he do? He stays out all night long and doesn't work, does he? Cola's gone. Grandfather's in the hospital. You want to know what the truth is? A certain person told me... *(Mara rises, clutches her sister's arms and shakes her.)* ...that we have to keep an eye on Antonio *(Shouting)* or else some day he'll do something foolish!

MARA *(continuing to shake Lucia)*: Who? Who told you that? Don Salvatore, wasn't it? And what's this?

She points to the necklace and tries to rip it from Lucia's neck.

LUCIA: It's nothing, nothing. Leave it alone, it's mine!

Mara slaps her.

MARA: Oh! It's yours, is it? *(Lucia breaks away, accidentally hitting the table as she runs by and sending the lamp crashing to the floor; Mara catches her by the hair.)* Shameful creature! Shameful creature!

LUCIA: Let me go! Let me go!

Mara tries to grab Lucia's necklace, but the younger girl breaks free again and escapes out the door. Outside, the sound of the harmonica grows louder. Lucia walks slowly across the courtyard. Mara falls weeping across the table.

Bastianello Alley. Day.

Lorenzo leans against the wall smoking; he seems to be waiting for someone. Antonio appears walking up the steep alley.

LORENZO: Hello, Antonio.

ANTONIO *(distracted)* : Hello.

He starts into the courtyard of his house, but Lorenzo addresses him again.

LORENZO: Haven't seen you for a while. How are you?

ANTONIO: All right, all right.

LORENZO: Don't you ever come down to the beach any more?
(Antonio enters the courtyard without answering.) ...Too bad
you don't go out fishing any more! You're a good fisherman, but if you stay home all the time, you'll forget it
all!... *(Antonio turns to listen.)* ...I've got a lot of boats
working for me... They go out every night...

ANTONIO: Not even if I die of hunger and the rest of my family
with me!

Courtyard of the Valastro house. Day.

Lorenzo comes toward Antonio.

LORENZO: You're still refusing? You're too proud, Antonio! See
what you've accomplished working on your own? And
you're still so stubborn?

ANTONIO *(shouting)* : I do what I want to! Leave me alone!

*He goes on into the courtyard. Lorenzo tosses away his cigarette and
follows him in.*

LORENZO: Are you shouting because maybe you have someone on
your side?

Enraged, Antonio starts back toward Lorenzo.

ANTONIO: Who? Who is this someone on my side?

In the background, an old woman sits working in her doorway.

LORENZO: I don't know, but they say Antonio Valastro's turned into a bum! He spends his days in the taverns and doesn't see what's going on in his own house!

Antonio grabs him by the shirt, shouting.

ANTONIO: You bastard! If we're poor it's your fault and your friends'! Get out! Get out of my house!

Antonio pushes Lorenzo up against the wall. Lorenzo throws him to the ground. The old woman in the background runs to the courtyard entrance screaming.

OLD WOMAN: Mara! Hurry, they're fighting! Don't kill each other!

Lorenzo hurls himself on Antonio; they wrestle on the ground as the neighbor women take up the cry. Finally Antonio frees himself and Lorenzo falls to the ground.

ANTONIO: Get out of my house! Get out of my house!

An old woman helps Lorenzo to his feet, shrieking.

OLD WOMAN: Antonio, what've you done? Are you trying to kill him?

Lorenzo stumbles off toward the alley with the old woman.

LORENZO: Don't worry, we'll meet again!

At the courtyard entrance, a disheveled woman shouts angrily at all the Valastros.

WOMAN: God's punished you for your pride! You're the worst family in Trezza now!

After a pause, Antonio sadly enters the house. Slow background music begins as the cries of the women fade.

Valastro house. Dining room. Day.

The musical background continues throughout the scene. Antonio enters, closes the door, and goes toward the table. Mara is standing beside the door, her arms folded. The mother and Lia stand by the table, which is empty save for a single sheet of paper.

MARA: Antonio! *(Coming to the table and gazing at the paper)* The eviction notice's come.

The document is from the Catania Magistrate's Court; it notifies the Valastros that they must leave their house "within ten days of receipt of this notice." The music fades.

Valastro house. Women's bedroom. Day.

Mara and the mother are folding a blanket. Lia sits on the bed cradling a doll. Mara goes to open the wardrobe and takes out some sheets.

MARA: Wait, Mother. Let's put these sheets in the chest too.

The mother holds the trunk lid open as Mara puts the sheets inside. Mara closes the trunk and looks toward the window, as the mother goes over to Lia. The workmen are heard outside.

MARA: Mother, I'm going out a minute; I'll be right back.

She goes out. The mother sits on the bed and carefully folds a dress. She places it on a blanket spread out on the floor and begins to roll up the bundle.

In front of the house. Day.

Mara approaches Nicola, who is working on a low wall. She looks at him sadly.

NICOLA: Is that you, Mara?

MARA: I've come to say goodbye.

A workman passes behind them with a bucket on his shoulder.

NICOLA: I'm glad you came to say goodbye, so I can say goodbye too. I heard you've got to leave today. Is that right?

Nicola puts down his trowel, jumps down from the wall, and comes toward Mara.

MARA: The bank's taken our house.

NICOLA: Well, goodbye. *(He glances at Mara's window.)* From now on I'll always be seeing your window closed... and my heart will close too.

Mara lowers her eyes sadly and leans against the wall.

MARA: It's God's will, Nicola!

NICOLA: God's will is bitter!

They walk slowly along. Jano watches them and then resumes his work, singing his favorite song through most of the scene.

JANO: We talk... we wrote...

Mara sits down on a little wall; Nicola stops in front of her.

MARA: When you finish this wall here, where will you go to work?

NICOLA: Wherever there is work. Now that it's winter there's no work here. I'll go to the city, to Catania or Syracuse.

He sits down beside her.

MARA: Well, goodbye, I have to go, my mother's waiting for me. Do you remember, Nicola... *(He nods.)* ...when you said we'd get rich and you were too poor to marry me? *(Mara lowers her eyes and pauses briefly before looking at him again.)* See how rich we are? We haven't even got a roof over our heads now!

NICOLA *(moved)*: It doesn't make any difference to me, Mara. If I could do what my heart tells me to, I know what I'd do.

MARA *(sad and resigned)* : Now things are different. I can't expect to marry any more. It's God's will. And now...

Nicola comes close to her.

NICOLA: I know you were born into a family better than mine, that you're the daughter of well-to-do people. *(He takes some nuts and the penknife from his pocket.)* And now that you have nothing left, I could take care of you with my muscles and my work. Forgive me, Mara, if I say these things to you.

He opens a nut and offers it to Mara, who takes it and holds it in her hand. Jano's song ends.

MARA: When you come back here, come around, to the house we're going to live in. Goodbye now, Nicola. *(Getting up)* I have to go now.

After a few uncertain steps she breaks into a run and disappears behind the curve of the steeply descending road.

Valastro house. Dining room. Dawn.

Vanni stands on a chair removing the Sacred Heart image from the wall. He calls to his mother, who is at the sideboard with the baby in her arms.

VANNI: Let's put this in the chest too.

He goes out as the mother takes the family portrait from the wall. The church bell is ringing. The mother sits down on a case with the photograph in her hands. Vanni is seen working in the courtyard.

Antonio sets the bedstead against the courtyard wall and looks around. Mara, carrying some household goods, stops and leans against a tree as Maccherone crosses the courtyard. Antonio comes over to Mara, who goes silently toward the pile of household furnishings in the center of the courtyard. A number of fishermen and friends of the Valastros are helping them move out. The mother goes out into the courtyard and sits down on a case. Antonio picks up a bedstead and speaks to his mother.

ANTONIO: Let's go, Mother.

She rises and follows him, with Mara and the others following behind.

Beach. Day.

Two beflowered boats are lined up on the beach. The villagers are celebrating. Lorenzo is at Nedda's side as she breaks a bottle of wine against one of the boats to christen it; another woman does the same to the other boat.

Shouts, applause and festive pealing of church bells. The priest moves between the boats with his aspersorium and blesses them. At the end of the operation all applaud and shout. Raimondo climbs up onto one of the boats, wildly applauded by the people, and bows to the crowd.

RAIMONDO: First of all we thank our noble lady Baroness... *(The aged Baroness is chewing candy behind her dark glasses as she sits beneath a black umbrella, surrounded by applauding villagers.)* ...who's been so kind as to come to the christening of our new boats. *(Panting, he wipes the sweat from his face and continues.)* These are the new boats for ten new crews, and they're almost ready! *(General applause)* Because here at Aci Trezza you're all good workers, except for a few who're sick in the head and want to do for themselves.

His last words are covered by laughter, shouts, and applause. The priest starts to leave. Nedda and Lorenzo are half-hidden behind the boat; Lorenzo removes a flower from the decorations and presents it to the girl.

RAIMONDO: Hurrah for the secretary! *(Shouts and applause)* We thank everybody in Trezza for coming to the christening of our boats!

A little girl brings him a tray of white candies, which Raimondo showers by the handful on the cheering crowd.

The Valastros' new home. Entrance. Outside. Day.

Antonio stands before the entrance; he turns, listening to the shouts and applause audible from the beach. Vanni is mending a small net. Antonio enters the house and lies down on a cot beside the door.

Beach. Day.

Surrounded by the festive crowd, Raimondo distributes the last of the candy.

Cliffs and road. Day.

Vanni and Alfio are returning home along the cliff; they have been fishing with their little nets. A peddler boy cries his wares beside a group of children. Some women are working in their doorways; hens wander around in the road.

Alley. Day.

Vanni and Alfio cross the alley and climb some steps. The peddler boy cries his wares along the alley, at the end of which an old woman sits unraveling a skein of yarn.

Drydock on the beach. Outside. Day.

A boat is being repaired. A woman is feeding a fire at the entrance. A little boy carrying a basket enters and goes up to the boat. A little girl, Rosa, runs up and hides at the entrance as if spying on someone. Sounds of workmen and of the sea.

Antonio comes up, hands in pockets; Rosa observes him. Two men are feeding another fire.

ROSA: Hello, Antonio.

BASTIANO: Hello, Antonio.

ANTONIO: Hello, Bastiano.

Antonio goes off as the little girl steps out. A carpenter is repairing the Valastro boat. His hammering is heard throughout the scene. Antonio walks around the boat, examines it attentively, and sits down on it. Rosa, who has been following him, watches him as she leans against the gunwale. Antonio turns and sees her.

ANTONIO: What do you want, little girl?

ROSA *(smiling)* : This is your boat, isn't it? And we're fixing it for you.

ANTONIO: Yes, you're fixing it for me, but I haven't got any money to pay you for it. Did you know that?

ROSA: Everybody says you're poor... *(She walks around the boat, climbs up onto it and sits facing Antonio.)* ... but in the village they hate you.

ANTONIO *(sadly)* : I know it.

Rosa leans on her elbow and makes herself comfortable.

ROSA: If I could help you... I would!

She smiles at Antonio. He looks at her with a bitter smile.

ANTONIO: Help me? How could you help me? The people who

could do it don't because they're so jealous. But they should've understood that I did what I did for everybody, not just for myself. And now? You see how they've all walked out on me? And they'd like to eat me alive! *(He turns to look at the boat; Rosa lowers her eyes; he turns back to her and slaps the boat.)* This has been in my family for ages! See how wrecked it is? Everybody says it was my fault it was wrecked. *(He stares into the distance and seems to be talking to himself.)* But some day they'll all realize I was right! Then it'll be a blessing for everybody to lose everything like I did! *(Turning back to Rosa)* We have to learn to stick up for each other, to stick together. Then we can go forward...

He jumps down from the boat and goes off slowly. Rosa remains seated and removes her kerchief. Then she jumps down, too, and follows Antonio. She stops a little distance behind him. Antonio turns.

ROSA: Antonio! Come back soon to see your boat!

Antonio goes off without answering, as Rosa sits down on the stones and watches him.

The Valastros' new home. Entrance. Outside. Day.

Alfio watches a woman cooking out in the alley; smoke is pouring from the little stove. Antonio appears, climbing up the embankment steps, and looks silently at his brother.

Vanni and Lia are sitting on the ground in front of the entrance. The mother sits with the baby in her arms. Mara kneels to wrap some garments in a tablecloth lying on the ground, as Antonio comes up to her. Everyone's eyes are on him. He picks up a scarf from the pile of clothing Mara is wrapping up.

ANTONIO: What're you going to do, sell it? Wait!

He goes into the house; Mara resumes her task.

Inside the new house. Day.

Slow sad music begins and continues throughout the scene. Antonio enters the house and pulls his navy chest from under the cot. He sets it on the bed and takes out his uniform, which he places in a towel along with his scarf, cap, and sweater. He puts on another, more ragged sweater and takes the bundle outside.

Outside the new house. Day.

Vanni sits in front of the door preparing a fishing pole. He calls his brother.

VANNI: Alfio! Come here! *(Alfio sits down beside Vanni.)* Don't look over there; it just makes you hungrier!

Antonio sits down between his brothers and caresses little Alfio's head; the boy gazes at him in silence.

Entrance to the co-operative. Outside. Day.

The co-op's sign reads: "Cyclops Company — Transportation and Sale of Fish." A line of fishermen waits to sign up for jobs. The village square is crowded right down to the beach. Antonio, Vanni, Alfio come up toward the crowded entranceway, where Nino and Lorenzo are standing.

NINO: Oh! Look who's here! Hunger brings the wolf from his lair! Let him through, let him through!

LORENZO: Quiet as mice! Quiet as mice!

NINO: Oh, Antonio! Come here, come here! Come on in!

Antonio and his brothers walk into the co-op.

Inside of co-op. Day.

Laughing, Lorenzo claps Antonio on the shoulder and pushes him over to Raimondo's table.

LORENZO: Look who's here, look who's here! *(Laughing)* Raimondo! The stray lamb's come back to the fold!

Raimondo rises, laughing.

RAIMONDO: Oh, Antonio! You're back? And you're the one who wanted to send the whole town to the bottom? *(He sits down again, laughing loudly.)* See how your bright ideas turn out? I've got to send out four new crews. You want to work? There's room for you! Want to sign up?

LA TERRA TREMA : 99

ANTONIO *(serious)* : Yes, I do want to sign up.

RAIMONDO: You want to sign up alone, or with some of your brothers?

He looks around with a vulgar laugh.

ANTONIO: Me and my brothers Vanni and Alfio as helpers.

Raimondo, leaning against the wall, continues to laugh.

RAIMONDO: Antonio! Here's the mother hen with her little chicks! Come on, come on! I'll take the whole family!

He laughs.

ANTONIO *(clenching his teeth)* : We know all about it!

Alfio watches, serious-faced. Raimondo looks at the boy; his laughter dies away and he turns to Lorenzo.

RAIMONDO: Lorenzo, sign them up in Domenico's crew! *(He raps his fist on the table.)* Is that all right with you, Antonio? You happy now?

ANTONIO: Yes, Domenico's crew's all right.

Lorenzo sits on the table as Antonio and his brothers go to sign up.

LORENZO: Go sign up. Antonio, didn't you tell me you wouldn't work for us even if you died of hunger and your whole family too?

Antonio stops short and looks at him in silence. Lorenzo and Raimondo suddenly turn serious.

ANTONIO *(to the clerk)* : Where do I sign?

CLERK: You sign here, for your brothers too. You get full wages.

Antonio is startled.

LORENZO: Next man!

Antonio looks toward Raimondo and Lorenzo.

CLERK: The crews are all full now. Your brother Vanni gets half pay and your brother Alfio gets a quarter, as helpers—all right?

Antonio looks at Alfio and after a pause turns back to sign. The clerk hands him three forms. Antonio goes toward the exit after signing. An old man steps up to the clerk after Antonio.

CLERK: Uncle Giovanni, you can row in Rosso's crew, and we'll give you full pay.

GIOVANNI: But what about the stern?

CLERK: You're an old man, what d'you want? If you want to complain, go to Raimondo!

Giovanni, grumbling, goes to Raimondo's table.

GIOVANNI: Raimondo, why didn't you give me the stern? This is wrong!

LORENZO: Next man!

RAIMONDO: Just thank God we're hiring you! You're another griper? Then go fish on your own and we'll see how you end up!

Antonio and his brothers go out the door, where Nino gives them an ironical military salute. Another fisherman enters. Lorenzo goes up to the new arrival and shows him the table.

LORENZO: You go over there! *(Another fisherman waits in front of the table; Lorenzo comes around to Raimondo, laughing.)* Raimondo! Here's another one who comes to us when he's dying of hunger!

Lorenzo laughs in the fisherman's face. Raimondo comes up to him.

RAIMONDO: Oh, Carmelo! When you're dying of hunger you come to us, eh? *(He pulls a piece of bread from his pocket and holds it up to Carmelo's mouth, laughing.)* Here's a piece of bread, Carmelo! Here, have a bite! Yum yum!

Nino comes over.

NINO: And it's so easy to get along with us, after all! *(He takes a piece of fruit from a cupboard and starts to peel it with his penknife.)* Raimondo! What do we want? We want to let everybody work so they can earn their bread! We want to help everybody!

He laughs. Two dealers sitting nearby laugh at Nino's humor.

LORENZO: Next man!

The Valastros' new house. Entrance. Day.

Mara helps Antonio, Vanni, and Alfio prepare for the night's fishing. Lia and the mother, who holds the baby, watch silently from the doorway.

ALFIO: Bless me, Mother.

VANNI: Bless me, Mother.

Mara gives Antonio the food and the bottle of wine.

MARA: Here, Antonio.

She ties his scarf around his neck as he gazes at the sky.

ANTONIO: Sister! It's good weather for anchovies! *(He comes over to his mother.)* Bless me, Mother.

MOTHER: God bless you.

He goes off as his mother and Mara walk to the little gate at the entrance. Mara then re-enters the house.

Inside the house. Day.

Mara takes the family portrait and hangs it on the wall beside the Sacred Heart. She passes a hand over the photograph, as if to caress the figures. Slow background music throughout the scene.

On the sea. Evening.

Antonio is standing up in the boat, looking straight ahead and rowing vigorously. His expression is harsh and painful. Vanni and the other fishermen are behind him.

VOICE: Come on, come on!

Calls and shouts. With their lanterns ablaze, the boats move out as the sails begin to pick up the wind. Sound of oars on water and voices of fishermen. On the screen appear the words: THE END.

Senso (1954)

Credits

Producer:	Domenico Forges Davanzati
Director:	Luchino Visconti
Screenplay:	Luchino Visconti, Suso Cocchi d'Amico, assisted by G. Prosperi, C. Alianello, G. Bassani, from a novella by Camillo Boito
Directors of Photography:	R. R. Aldo, Robert Krasker
Camera Operator:	Giuseppe Rotunno, Francesco Izzarelli
Art Directors:	Ottavio Scotti, Gino Brosio
Music:	Bruckner's Seventh Symphony, Verdi's *Il Trovatore*
Costumes:	Marcel Escoffier, Piero Tosi
Sound:	Vittorio Trentino

Venice. Spring 1866.

The last months of the Austrian occupation of the Venetian provinces. The Italian government has concluded an alliance with Prussia and the "War of Liberation" is imminent.

The stage of the Venice Theater in Venice, during the performance of Act III of "Il Trovatore."

Manrico advances to the footlights and sings "Di quella pira..."

The orchestra and the balconies are crowded with Austrian officers and Italian civilians. In the orchestra, Ussoni walks forward, followed by another patriot. They mingle with the standing audience. Ussoni looks up toward the balconies.

A patriot removes a packet of tricolored leaflets from his coat and cautiously passes them to a girl. The pamphlets pass from hand to hand. Someone hands several bunches of tricolored flowers to a girl. Another girl removes some more flowers from under her cloak, where they had been pinned to her crinoline.

On stage, the third act draws to a close. Manrico, at the footlights, turns toward the rear, followed by his soldiers. The audience in the balconies breaks into wild applause. In the orchestra, the impassive expression of the Austrian officers contrasts with the civilians' enthusiasm.

A girl throws a bunch of tricolored flowers from the top balcony to the orchestra.

GIRL: All foreigners out of Venice!

It hits an Austrian soldier on the shoulder. The soldier picks up the flowers,

gazes at them with disdain, and then turns to look up toward the balcony. The pamphlets rain down.

MAN: Venetians, La Marmora has begun to march!

VOICES: Hurrah for La Marmora! Hurrah for Italy! Hurrah for Italy!

The people in the balconies warm to the demonstration of their feelings of Italian nationality. The pamphlets continue to rain down in increasing numbers on the orchestra, where the Austrian officers have remained seated at the end of the act while the civilians have risen enthusiastically to their feet.

Two stagehands come out from the wings during the intermission. One of them catches one of the pamphlets as it falls and bends down to pick up another. The musicians have risen to go out during the intermission. They look toward the balconies. Several bend down to pick up the pamphlets.

VOICES: Hurrah for Verdi! Hurrah for Italy! Hurrah for Free Venice! Hurrah for La Marmora! Hurrah for Verdi!

Count Serpieri appears at one of the stage boxes.

SERPIERI *(in German)* : Where is the Security Police? It's an absolute disgrace! *(He turns to the general, who is behind him.)* Just look at that, general! I think that if things go on like this... *(The general appears from the rear and looks with Serpieri toward the orchestra.)* ...there's only one thing to do: empty the theater. Please look at that, general!

The Austrian general walks off with Count Serpieri. Livia comes toward the next bay of the stage box and stops to look toward the orchestra. In the orchestra, a group of patriots moves forward among the still seated Austrian officers. Livia seems to be looking for someone. Down among the audience in the orchestra, Ussoni is taking part in the demonstration. He sees Livia and tosses her a bunch of tricolored flowers. Livia catches it and lifts it to her lips.

A group of Austrian officers observes the demonstration. One of them, Lieutenant Franz Mahler, is amusedly twirling a bunch of flowers in his fingers.

FRANZ: How entertaining! This is the kind of war that suits the Italians: showers of confetti to the sound of mandolins.

Ussoni turns in resentment at the Austrian's words.

USSONI: Coward! You're a coward! I'll show you how Italians fight! *(He puts his hand in his pocket.)* And if you're a gentleman...

He slaps the lieutenant on the face with his gloves. Mahler stares at him for a moment and then walks nonchalantly away.

VOICE OF A PATRIOT: Let me go!

Two guards appear, dragging along an Italian patriot.

PATRIOT: You haven't any right to touch me! *(He shouts in Mahler's face.)* Hurrah for Italy! Hurrah for Italian Venice! Hurrah for La Marmora!

The guards drag the patriot along, but as if by prearrangement, Ussoni and other patriots throw themselves on the guards in an attempt to free him. Mahler stops for a moment to watch and then moves on with disdainful nonchalance.

Livia is anxiously following the struggle from the box. She leaves the rail and walks resolutely toward the exit, but her husband cuts her off.

SERPIERI: Where are you going?

LIVIA: I'm going down to the foyer. It's suffocating here!

SERPIERI: I don't think this is the proper time.

LIVIA: Leave me alone. You know I'll do what I want to anyway!

SERPIERI: Anyway I won't allow you to go with those flowers.

He removes the flowers from the bosom of Livia's dress. Livia looks at him for a moment and then leaves. Count Serpieri follows her with his eyes.

Livia passes through the crowd of other women in the corridor. The ovations, shouts, and applause fade into a distant murmur.

LIVIA'S VOICE: Everything began that evening. It was the twenty-seventh of May.

Livia leans over the stairs and seems to be looking for someone in the foyer, which is crowded with officers and civilians.

LIVIA'S VOICE: My cousin, Roberto Ussoni, had been one of the organizers of the demonstration, and was also one of the leaders of the clandestine movement in Venice. I was very worried for him because he had senselessly exposed himself by challenging that officer.

She looks around her and hurries downstairs.

LIVIA'S VOICE: I was already trying to think of some way to help him.

Roberto Ussoni is talking excitedly with a group of Italians. Livia comes up to him.

LIVIA: Roberto!

USSONI: Livia!

Ussoni steps out of the group and presses her hand to his lips.

LIVIA: You were mad to do that! To expose yourself so openly. *(Ussoni smiles to reassure her.)* You shouldn't have done it!

USSONI: I don't know if it was right or wrong, but I couldn't help myself. When that devil said what he did...

LIVIA: And now what are you going to do?

USSONI: He's accepted the challenge. *(Ussoni leads her a few steps away.)* At least he seemed to. I'll fight him!

LIVIA: No, it's impossible! An officer, with the kind of situation you're in... It would have awful consequences. Something must be done. Get out of here. You've got to leave the theater right away! Go home, or to Massenga's, or Arrivabene's, or wherever you think. But wait till I let you know something. Please, please, Roberto, you've got to be careful... for everybody's sake!

Ussoni kisses her hand again.

USSONI: I know. Don't worry. But did you see how they pitched in this evening? There's a lot of work still to be done, but they're waking up, they're waking up!

A friend of Roberto's appears.

MENEGHINI: Come on, Roberto! Let's go, we'll go by the boat landing.

LIVIA: Goodbye, Roberto, go, go.

USSONI: Goodbye, Livia.

He kisses her hand again.

LIVIA: Go, go!

USSONI: Goodbye!

Ussoni leaves, followed by his friends.

The Austrian general leafs through some of the tricolored pamphlets. Two other officers are standing nearby, along with Count Serpieri.

COLONEL *(in German)* : That looks like an appeal from "La Marmora." We certainly haven't published it in our newspapers. But that's absolutely senseless! And now the people of Venice are getting stirred up even more. Well, there are a lot of people in Venice who are not in the least bit moved by "La Marmora" and her "provocations." *(The colonel turns to Count Serpieri, to whom he speaks in Italian.)* It's really such a pity that we have to give up our music, my dear Count... but we cannot allow the Venice Theater to become a stage for revolutionary demonstrations!

SERPIERI: I'm the first to agree with you, but I beg your Excellency to believe me when I assure you that this is the action of some agent provocateur, no doubt about it.

GENERAL: Yes, it's really a beautiful evening this evening!

The musicians begin to tune up. The Austrian general's wife and daughter are in Serpieri's box. Livia returns from the foyer. The general's wife sits down on a small sofa.

GENERAL'S WIFE: Ah, Countess Serpieri, there's going to be a duel, really there is! *(Livia sits on a small bench beside her.)* Someone's challenged Franz Mahler. *(The Austrian lady laughs in amusement.)* Perhaps they're going to settle the "Venetian question." *(She laughs again.)* And you are well acquainted with the challenger, Countess!

Serpieri enters and comes over to the general's wife.

SERPIERI: Please, my lady, let's not speak of this unpleasant incident. The young man is a distant relative of ours but we never see him. Anyway, the people one knows least well are always... one's relatives.

LIVIA: I know him very well. No, my lady, it's not the "Venetian question." My cousin is not interested in politics; he's absolutely uninterested, really apathetic, as far as politics is concerned, I mean. There must be some other reason. That lieutenant... Mahler... *(She rises and walks toward the general.)* There's a lot of talk about him.

GENERAL: I'm sure there is. All the ladies of Venice talk about him.

LIVIA: That must be it, they must have had words over a woman. That's the way history is falsified. Don't you agree?

The general and the colonel laugh in agreement.

GENERAL: Ja!

LIVIA: Is the officer under your command, Excellency?

COLONEL: Mahler? *Gewiss!*

GENERAL: Yes, yes, indeed.

LIVIA: You know, I should like very much to meet him. Since all the ladies of Venice are talking about him... I'd like very much to talk about him too!

GENERAL: Countess, this is a favor you shouldn't be asking of an admirer. Lieutenant Mahler is too dangerous a rival!

The general motions a young officer over and murmurs in his ear. The officer goes off.

The opera music begins again.

GENERAL: Would you like to sit here?

LIVIA: No, no, thank you, Excellency. *(Livia goes over to look in the mirror; we see her image reflected in the mirror.)* "Trovatore" is nothing new for me. And you Austrians love music, but we Italians go to the theater for entirely different reasons.

The fourth act of "Trovatore" begins on stage.

Franz Mahler appears at the entrance to the box, salutes with a snap of his head, and enters. The general introduces Mahler to Livia.

GENERAL: Countess... Lieutenant Mahler... Countess Serpieri.

Mahler remains at attention. Livia invites him to sit beside her on the sofa.

LIVIA: Please sit down.

Mahler sits down next to Livia.

FRANZ: Thank you.

LIVIA: Can you see well enough?

FRANZ: Quite well... Quite well, thank you.

LIVIA: Do you like opera, Lieutenant Mahler?

FRANZ: Yes, I like opera very much, Countess Serpieri... when I like the opera... and you?

LIVIA: Of course, I like it very much. I don't care for it offstage, though, or for people who act like melodramatic heroes... without considering the consequences...of an impulsive gesture... or of some unpardonable thoughtlessness. May I speak frankly?

FRANZ: Please do. I don't think much of any other way of talking.

LIVIA: If I have heard correctly, there is to be a duel tomorrow, isn't there? And you're the one who has to decide whether or not to accept the challenge, aren't you? I'm curious to know.

Mahler laughs.

FRANZ: I'm very curious to know myself.

LIVIA: Don't take up the challenge. It's not right to expose one's life that way.

FRANZ: Why should you be concerned about my life?

LIVIA: It's a matter of principle.

FRANZ: Don't worry about it. Neither my life nor your principles are in danger. This stupid incident will end soon with a pair of handcuffs.

LIVIA: What do you mean?

FRANZ: Splendid music! Will you be here tomorrow evening? If you are, may I come back?

Livia covers her shoulders with her veil.

LIVIA: I don't feel well... I must leave! *(She rises suddenly, followed by the young officer.)* Please, don't leave. *(She goes to the general, who rises to say goodbye.)* Goodbye, Excellency.

GENERAL: Countess, you're already depriving us of your company?

LIVIA: I feel a little ill!

GENERAL: I'm terribly sorry to hear it.

LIVIA: Good evening. *(She passes through the group of Austrian officers; Count Serpieri comes toward her.)* Let's go.

SERPIERI: But if you don't feel well, perhaps you ought to wait a little.

LIVIA: Let's go.

SERPIERI: As you like.

He goes out. The general's wife comes up to Livia.

GENERAL *(in German)*: Goodbye, Countess, are you going so soon? Come and hear "Die Freischutz" with us again.

LIVIA *(in German)*: Good evening.

Serpieri returns with Livia's cape and places it over her shoulders. One of the officers kisses the countess's hand. Serpieri says goodbye to the general and the colonel.

SERPIERI: Excellency! Colonel.

The general's wife is conversing in German with an officer. Livia and her husband leave. The general's wife, enchanted by the music, goes up to the box rail and breaks into phrases of admiration.

The entranceway of the Serpieri mansion.

Livia and her husband enter. A footman approaches with a torch. Livia approaches the two patriots who are awaiting her.

LOREDAN: They've just arrested Roberto, as he was leaving the theater.

LIVIA: No, it's impossible!

ARRIVABÉNE: He was with Porrà and Meneghini. They arrested all of them.

LIVIA: Something must be done... right away!

LOREDAN: Why don't you ask your husband? If he pulls some strings...

LIVIA: Let me take care of it. You've got to go now. Tell Massenga. I'll let you know. But please leave here right away. Don't take any chances. Good night.

LOREDAN: Good night.

ARRIVABENE: Good night.

Livia comes up to her husband as the two patriots go out another door.

LIVIA: Did you hear? They've arrested Roberto. Listen, I've never asked you for anything, but this time you must do something...to free Roberto! If you want to...with the people you know, with all the friends you have... It must have been that lieutenant who denounced him, I'm sure of it. He didn't want to fight!

SERPIERI: I'm sure he didn't! How could you think that an Austrian officer could fight an Italian civilian? It would be perfectly absurd! *(The count motions to the footman, who starts up the stairs.)* If your cousin had an ounce of good sense in his head...

LIVIA: You know what this can mean at this time.

SERPIERI: Yes, I know perfectly well, and I don't want anything to do with this business! They were perfectly right to arrest him! You want me to compromise myself with these goings-on that don't interest me in the least?! I'm fed up with them! Don't speak of it again, understand? They're just a bunch of adolescent pranks. *(Livia turns abruptly from him and starts up the stairs; Serpieri follows her.)* I wonder what they think they're going to accomplish!

Livia is bidding farewell to Ussoni, who has been sentenced to exile.

LIVIA'S VOICE: Roberto was sentenced to a year in exile, along with many others. *(The two walk a few paces away from a large group of patriots waiting to be called.)* I had a strange foreboding... of what his departure might mean... for me.

Roberto kisses Livia's hand. His name is called.

USSONI: Farewell. *(He bends to kiss her hand once more.)* Let's hope it's not for long, my guardian angel. *(He looks warily about.)* Try to get to Aldeno as soon as you can.

LIVIA: Yes, yes.

USSONI: Be sure to let Cavalletto know.

LIVIA: Don't worry.

USSONI: We need a safe link with the partisan bands. I hope I can get there soon. Garibaldi's at Desenzano. Just think, Livia, the time is drawing near! Farewell... Italians!

He kisses her on the cheeks. Again he presses her hand and kisses it.

LIVIA: Roberto... be careful!

AUSTRIAN OFFICER: *Achtung! Abteilung 'arsch!*

The officer walks away along the portico where the prisoners are waiting. Ussoni rejoins the group of prisoners, who move off two by two to the commands of an Austrian soldier. Livia covers herself with her veil and waves goodbye as Ussoni passes by.

Livia hurries along from the rear of the portico, passing among soldiers and civilians. Franz Mahler is standing in one corner among a group of Austrian officers.

LIVIA'S VOICE: But when I saw that officer again... I realized that he...was the cause of my apprehensions...and that for many days I had been afraid of meeting him.

When Livia reaches the group of Austrian officers, Mahler turns.

FRANZ: Countess Serpieri!

Livia stops and Franz comes up to her. He greets her, touching his fingers to his visor.

LIVIA: What do you want?

FRANZ: May I escort you through this part of town?

LIVIA: No thank you, Lieutenant Mahler.

FRANZ: But there's a curfew in Venice and it's already very late!

LIVIA: Perhaps you wish to arrest me because I'm out after the curfew?

FRANZ: I've never had anyone arrested for such trivial infractions of the regulations!

LIVIA: What do you think of Roberto Ussoni's arrest?

FRANZ: Oh... was he arrested? I thought they were just going to give him a change of air for a while.

LIVIA: They've exiled him, and you know it.

FRANZ: You think it's my fault. But I assure you you're mistaken. I hope you'll believe me. And anyway, that Ussoni must be delighted about it! He seems to be the type who's born to sacrifice himself for some noble cause!

LIVIA: And what were you born for?

Franz laughs in amusement.

FRANZ: To be what I am.

LIVIA: To be what you are. Good evening.

Livia walks away. Franz runs after her.

FRANZ: Don't you think it would have been much better if you'd told me the other evening at the opera that Ussoni was your lover? And that you wanted me to do all I could to keep him in Venice?

LIVIA: A man with a minimum of good breeding would not take advantage of the fact that I'm alone to insult me.

Franz laughs. Livia walks on and Franz follows her a few paces behind.

Riello quay and bridge.

Music begins. Livia walks up onto the bridge and removes her veil as she reaches the center. Franz follows her along the quay, almost hidden from view. She stops and turns as he nears her. End of music.

LIVIA: I've already asked you not to follow me.

FRANZ: But I'm not following you.

Livia walks on, followed by Franz. She stops once more.

LIVIA: Ah, you're not following me?

FRANZ: Consider me your shadow.

LIVIA: Thanks, I already have one.

Livia continues on but stops again at the sound of Mahler's voice.

FRANZ: Mine will protect you much better.

LIVIA: Will you stop following me!

She hurries along but suddenly stops, terrified at the sight of the body of an Austrian soldier lying on the ground. Franz bends over the body and raises the head.

LIVIA: But... is he dead?

Franz, still bending over, holds the corpse in his arms.

FRANZ: Yes.

He lays it gently down again.

LIVIA: But how...

Franz interrupts her, motioning her to silence.

FRANZ: Shh!

They hear the sound of marching footsteps. Franz rises, takes Livia's arm and pulls her behind an arch.

FRANZ: Quick, over here! ... Come here, quick!

He covers her face with her veil. A five-man Austrian patrol approaches from the other end of the street. One of the soldiers sees the corpse. The patrol leader bends over it. (The following exchanges are in German.)

SOLDIER: Sergeant!

SERGEANT: Yes! What's the matter?

SOLDIER: Look over here!

SERGEANT: Good heavens! Is he dead? Quick! Take him away! Step forward two men. These damned Venetians. Every night they kill somebody like this! Come on! Let's go! The first one take the front, the other one the back.

The soldiers pick up the corpse and carry it away under the portico of the quay.

SERGEANT: Quick, quick, quick!

FIRST SOLDIER: Poor devil!

SECOND SOLDIER: I knew him. Only a little while ago he... And he arrived in Venice such a short time ago!

Livia and Franz breathe in relief. Livia removes her veil.

LIVIA: Thanks!

Music begins. She starts to walk off. Franz follows her.

FRANZ: You can see that... *(Livia stops.)* ...it's not very pleasant to be part of an army of occupation. One has to live among people who hate one. And as for us younger men, far from home, all alone, we end up courting their wives and their daughters.

LIVIA: Yes, I understand. Good evening, Lieutenant, I'm not afraid anymore. Please don't trouble yourself anymore. Good evening! *(Livia walks off, leaving the archway after a moment's hesitation; but after a few steps she stops and turns toward Franz.)* But there's one thing I'd like you to know. *(Franz comes up to her.)* Roberto Ussoni is not my lover.

FRANZ: Ah!

LIVIA: He's my cousin. And he's the person I admire most in this world.

FRANZ: You admire him more than your husband?

LIVIA: My husband and I have quite different opinions of the

Austrians. He tends to accept them and even asks favors of them. I'm like my cousin... a true Italian. Good evening.

Livia starts off. Franz remains fixed for a moment and then follows her.

FRANZ: Countess Serpieri...

They disappear one after the other around the corner.

Venice at night.

Livia walks on, still followed at a short distance by Franz.

LIVIA'S VOICE: We walked together for a long time, along the deserted streets. Time had stopped. There was only the secret pleasure I felt in listening to his talk, in hearing his laugh...

The well in the Ghetto Square.

LIVIA'S VOICE: ...and listening to the sound of our footsteps echoing in the silent city.

The couple walks up and stops by the well.

LIVIA: But where are we going?

FRANZ: Wherever you like.

LIVIA: I don't know at all. I don't know where we are.

Franz leans against the well.

FRANZ: We've gotten somewhere. *(Points to a house)* That's my house. I live there.

LIVIA: All by yourself?

FRANZ: No. No, not by myself, with some other officers. We often sit around in shirt sleeves, drinking beer and gossiping about women. But that'll all be different now.

LIVIA: Why?

FRANZ: Because I've met you.

A moment of silence. Franz picks up a piece of broken mirror from the ground.

LIVIA: What have you found?

FRANZ: A bit of mirror.

He sits on the edge of the well, looking at himself in the mirror.

LIVIA: Why are you looking at yourself that way? Do you like to look at yourself?

FRANZ: Yes, I do. I never pass a mirror without looking at myself.

LIVIA: Why do you like it so?

FRANZ: I like to look at myself to be sure I'm... me!

LIVIA: You're certain of it only then?

FRANZ: No. Also when I see a woman... looking at me the way you're looking at me right now. *(He pitches the bit of mirror away.)*

"'Tis the Judgment Day!
"The dead rise to eternal joy, or to eternal pain.
"We still embrace, heedless of all, both Paradise and Hell."

Do you like these lines of Heine's?

LIVIA: No.

The music ends. Franz is still seated on the edge of the well; Livia stands near him.

FRANZ: Why not?

LIVIA: It's the meaning I don't like.

Franz smiles.

FRANZ: That's a shame! But when a war's on hand...

LIVIA: You think there'll be war?

FRANZ: Oh, yes. *(He comes up to Livia.)* Even though it's inconceivable that people can kill each other over things that don't concern them at all. Do you believe in war?

LIVIA: I believe that the liberty of a people has to be defended even at the cost of one's own liberty... or life.

FRANZ: So we'll be enemies then, won't we? *(Franz puts his hand on Livia's.)* I don't believe it for a minute. I suppose it's a serious failure on my part, but I've never been able to get excited over war, or politics, or borderlines, or occupations of territory... all those extremely serious things that men are supposed to be ready to die for. You see, I think that even though people may be born one on one side of this river, and another on the other side of that mountain, that doesn't mean that God made rivers and mountains to keep them apart.

LIVIA: You're talking like a child. I don't understand how you can be a soldier with that kind of idea. It's ridiculous for you to be an officer!

Franz comes very close to Livia.

FRANZ: Yes, I agree with you. It's ridiculous. *(He caresses her shoulder almost playfully.)* It's all quite ridiculous.

Livia is quite troubled. The music begins again.

LIVIA: I must go now. It's almost dawn.

FRANZ: Livia... That's your name, isn't it?

LIVIA: Yes.

FRANZ: When may I see you again? Tomorrow?

LIVIA: No. It's impossible!

FRANZ: I'll wait.

Livia breaks away.

Workmen are unloading baskets of fish and vegetables from boats tied up at the Cannaregio quay. Franz and Livia walk along.

LIVIA'S VOICE: By then it was dawn. The city was waking up. And now I felt almost a sense of shame. How could I have spent the whole night out with a man I didn't know, an Austrian, an officer? I was an Italian woman, and married. A woman who'd never been flighty in her whole life.

Livia walks on alone as Franz stops, watching her.

The Ghetto Square.

Livia approaches the square from the bridge over the canal. She looks fearfully about her and walks rapidly across the square.

LIVIA'S VOICE: And yet, four days later, four endless days of hoping in vain to meet him, four days later I was running to him. *(Livia crosses the New Ghetto Square and approaches Franz's house; two Austrian officers stop to watch her.)* I'd been able to persuade myself... that he was the only one who could help Roberto. It was my duty to ask him to!

Livia opens the door resolutely as the music ends. She walks up the narrow stairway leading to Franz's apartment. An Austrian officer is whistling as he walks down the next flight of stairs; he stops to look at the woman, as does another officer who has appeared in a doorway facing the landing.

Franz's servant hurries whistling out of another doorway. He stops as he meets Livia, looks at her, and continues on down. Two officers look curiously at Livia from downstairs.

AN OFFICER: *Das ist eine Puppe, was?*

Livia stops before the door the servant has come out of and looks inside the room. It is a large room; the furniture and objects are in great disorder. An Austrian officer is seated at the central table, laying out a hand of solitaire. In a back corner of the room Franz finishes lighting an oil lamp and becomes aware of Livia's presence. He walks toward her.

BOHEMIAN OFFICER: Hey, do you want to play?

Franz's glance reveals Livia's presence to him. The Bohemian throws the deck of cards on the table, rises, takes his jacket from the back of his chair, and walks toward his room. Smiling, Franz continues forward with his eyes fixed on Livia.

Livia stands in the doorway. Franz approaches her, bends to kiss her hand tenderly, and leads her into the room as the Bohemian comes to the door after throwing his jacket on his bed.

FRANZ: I've waited days and days for you. And now you've come!

Franz throws the Bohemian a glance, and the latter slams the door disdain-

fully. Franz takes Livia's veil and lifts it slowly. He bends to give her a brief kiss. He looks at her.

FRANZ: We heed not Heaven or Hell.

A long kiss unites them once again.

Rio Noale.

Music begins. A gondola passes by.

LIVIA'S VOICE: After that day we met often. We went to a rented room Franz had found at the New Quay.

Franz and Livia sitting in the double bed.

LIVIA: Will you get me the brush?

FRANZ: Yes.

Franz gets up and walks to the dresser.

LIVIA: You see, if they told me, "You've got only the present. You have no tomorrow; you won't have a tomorrow" after this moment, I'd feel as if a doctor had told me... *(Franz returns with a brush and sits at the foot of the bed.)* ..."You're going to die. You've only got a few hours to live." *(Livia begins to brush her hair.)* And now I know it's true. We've only got "now," Franz. There's no tomorrow.

FRANZ: Every time you leave you say, "Farewell, Franz. We'll never see each other again." But every time I wait for you with the same faith. You may think you'll never see me again, but I keep on waiting for you.

Franz is stretched out, propped up on one elbow, as Livia braids her hair.

LIVIA: Perhaps...you will... *(She slips out of bed, covering herself with the sheet, and goes behind the baseboard of the bed to caress*

Franz's hair; he kisses her hand.) But you've had so many adventures... *(She walks away.)* ...where there was the noise of a moth in the room, or the buzz of a fly beating against the windows, and you realized it only afterwards, and you got up... and freed that poor trapped insect... *(The music ends.)* ...with the same elegance with which you freed yourself from the woman's heart. *(Livia finishes getting dressed; she has already put on her skirt and corset and she moves toward Franz.)* But don't worry. *(Franz rises to his knees in the bed, picks up the ends of the corset laces, and helps Livia tighten them.)* In this adventure, you won't have to make even that little effort. I'll do it for you, Franz. *(He gets down from the bed and comes over to Livia.)* I'll get up myself, I'll open the windows... and let your heart fly away, free as a butterfly. *(Franz plays with her hair.)* Would you please get me those little scissors?

Franz laughs.

FRANZ: Madame, I shall be your servant no longer. You'll have to get them yourself.

Livia leaves him and walks to the dresser. She rebraids her hair, but a sudden impulse makes her take a pair of scissors and cut off a lock, which she then places inside a precious medallion.

The music begins again. Franz looks out the window. He turns as Livia comes up to him and hands him the medallion.

LIVIA: Franz... take this to remember me by.

Franz admires the medallion, swinging it between his fingers.

FRANZ: What a splendid medallion!

LIVIA: Here, over your heart. Now I'm going... I'm going!

Franz bows quickly to kiss her hand.

FRANZ: Farewell. *(With the same superficiality he kisses her mouth.)* Farewell.

Livia moves slowly away from him as Franz continues to admire the medallion. But she turns.

LIVIA *(passionately)*: Oh, Franz, are you letting me just go off like this?

FRANZ: Of course not, my love. *(He comes up to her.)* I knew you wouldn't go.

He embraces and kisses her. The music fades and is replaced by the sound of bells.

Livia is walking up and down in the room. She looks around. She approaches the bed.

LIVIA'S VOICE: One afternoon as I waited for him in vain in that room, for the first time I realized, in terror, that I was no longer in control of my feelings... as I'd imagined!

As she hears the door open, Livia, reassured, turns toward it and sees the landlady.

LANDLADY: I have to go out a minute, but there's no one here; what shall I do, leave the door open? Or will you go down and open it?

LIVIA: But you're sure the lieutenant left no message...or note?

LANDLADY: Well! Of course not, madame!

LIVIA: But perhaps you were out and no one was here.

LANDLADY: Oh, what can I say? Maybe he's gone away. *(The landlady closes the door.)* There was a captain who used to come here all the time, and he was suddenly transferred... Come to think of it, madame, do you know anyone who could help me? You know what they're going to do? They want to requisition my house for army quarters! I say, don't they have barracks for that? Madame, see if you can help me. For your sake too. I know you can if you try, Countess Serpieri... I know you very well, you know. My sister worked for you for a long time. *(Livia hurries to the door and opens it.)* What? Are you leaving now? Suppose the lieutenant comes. *(Livia re-enters.)* Listen, madame. *(She closes the door again.)* Suppose the lieutenant really has gone away. Who's to pay here? You know I've never asked for anything because I know him so well, but... *(Livia opens her purse.)* You know, just for the linens, madame. *(Livia hands her some money.)* Oh. Thank you, madame! *(Livia opens the door and goes out.)* Oh my!

Inside Franz's apartment, a very young officer reclines on a sofa in one corner of the large room, absorbed in his own thoughts. His comrades are singing. Livia appears at the door, which has been left ajar.

One of the officers is putting on his shoes. Livia moves toward the center of the room. Two officers are playing cards at the central table. Another officer lies on the sofa at the back of the room, while another is busy writing next to him. A sixth, Hintermann, appears with a book in hand. No one notices Livia.

LIVIA: Excuse me. Is Lieutenant Mahler here?

The singing stops; only one man continues to sing softly.

LIVIA: But is he still in Venice?

OFFICER: Yes, he's still in Venice.

LIVIA: Do you know when he'll be back?

OFFICER: I can't tell you that, madame.

LIVIA: I'll wait for him.

OFFICER: Make yourself comfortable.

The officer lying on the sofa gets up.

BOHEMIAN: Please sit down, miss. Do you like our place?

Livia does not answer.

HINTERMANN: She doesn't say she likes it, but she comes all the same.

All the men laugh. Livia walks toward Franz's room as the men begin to sing again.

SERVANT: Two pairs of shorts... three shirts... two good shirts... and two sheets. *(Livia approaches the servant, who is checking Franz's laundry with the washerwoman.)* All right. My master will stop by tomorrow to pay the bill.

He slaps the washerwoman's behind.

WASHERWOMAN: Keep your paws down! Damn you!

She leaves with the basket under her arm. The Bohemian is in the doorway.

LIVIA: But the lieutenant didn't tell you where he was going?

SERVANT: How should I know? He didn't come back last night.

LIVIA: He was out... all night?

SERVANT: Not the whole night, that's for sure.

LIVIA: But he didn't come back this morning? You didn't see him?

SERVANT: How should I know? Maybe he was at Katy's or at Nana's.

The servant laughs. The Bohemian enters and crosses the room.

LIVIA: Who said so?

SERVANT: Well, if you want to wait, go right ahead!

He moves away.

LIVIA: But you're sure he's not nearby? Or at the barracks?

The Bohemian comes over to Livia.

BOHEMIAN: He sure isn't here. I can guarantee that. It's the only thing I can guarantee you. But if you're patient... *(Livia walks to the rear of the room.)* ...and seeing you're a friend of Franz's... *(One of the Austrians is in the doorway.)* ...you sure must be!

HINTERMANN: Ludwig says he was with Franz an hour ago, playing billiards. We don't know where he went afterwards.

BOHEMIAN: You can't keep your mouth shut, can you? Don't listen to him. He doesn't know what he's saying himself. Why don't you sit down? Franz'll be here soon. Even if no one ever knows what he's up to or where he goes... *(Livia sits down on a little sofa next to the dressing table.)* He's always out somewhere, you never know where. What can you do? That's the way he is! Once we lived three months together in the same...

Livia's hand moves slowly along the top of the dressing table, where Franz has left the lock of hair she gave him. The medallion is missing. She squeezes the lock between her fingers.

BOHEMIAN: ...apartment. In Innsbruck. I spent the whole day receiving girls who came to look for him. And even if he was there he didn't want to see them.

The music fades.

Livia walks up the stairway leading to the drawing room of the Serpieri mansion. The maid approaches her.

LAURA: Madame.

LIVIA: What is it?

LAURA: We're leaving.

LIVIA: Who says so?

LAURA: The master is giving orders to pack things away!

LIVIA: You must have misunderstood. *(Livia continues quickly up the stairs.)* What's going on? *(She crosses the drawing room, where the servants are removing the furniture; she approaches her husband.)* You might have told me. Or do you consider me...

SERPIERI: The Prussians have occupied Austrian Holstein. This means the war has started, and I think it prudent...

LIVIA: No, it's not possible! Just like that, on a moment's notice.

SERPIERI: What do you expect?

LAURA: Your orders, madame?

LIVIA: There's time, Laura, there's time!

Livia sits down on a sofa next to the wall.

LIVIA'S VOICE: My husband's decision appalled me. But I was able to persuade him to put off our departure for at least... *(Serpieri sits down beside his wife.)* ... twenty-four hours.

The Arsenal Square.

Trumpets are sounding. Livia runs across the wooden bridge leading to the Arsenal Square and goes toward the building through groups of Austrian officers. She approaches two officers standing on the steps of the arsenal. Bells ring.

LIVIA: Lieutenant Mahler, please, of the Eighth Company.

OFFICER: The Eighth Company isn't here any more. They're at the Misericordia barracks.

Trumpets. Livia goes off.

Entrance to the Serpieri mansion.

The bell rings. A servant runs to open the door. Livia enters, exhausted and disheveled. She walks like an automaton. The music begins. Laura hurries down the stairs carrying an umbrella. She meets Livia.

LAURA: Oh, madame. I was going to look for you and bring you an umbrella. The master told me to. But where was I to go? You didn't tell me where you were going. I'd have tried Countess Marcella's, or the marquise... Oh! You're all wet! What weather! It certainly doesn't feel like summer. Even the sky's gone mad, because of the war. I remember so well how it was in '59. The master was worried. I said you must have had to do something. When she goes out... There was a man who came to look for you too, someone I'd never seen before. No, I didn't say anything to the master. He says you must go right away to a certain person in San Geremia Square No. 349 and ring three times.

LIVIA: When did he come? Who was it?

LAURA: I don't know. You'd just gone out. I told you... I was going to look for you...

LIVIA: I'll be back later! Give me the umbrella!

The music ends. She hurries toward the door.

LAURA: What shall I tell the master?

Livia opens the door.

LIVIA: Whatever you like! I don't care! I don't care about anything, you understand? Tell him everything if you want! Tell him.

She slams the door behind her. Music begins.

Laura turns as she hears someone coming down the stairs behind her. It is Serpieri. He stops a moment as if to ask her something, then continues on.

Serpieri opens the door and looks outside for his wife. He seems to have seen her. He follows her along a street, keeping out of sight.

Livia runs up a flight of stairs toward a landing. Serpieri, unseen, follows immediately after. Livia reaches the landing and rings three times at the door. Serpieri runs up to her. As soon as Livia sees him she backs against the wall.

LIVIA: You didn't have to follow me... to find out. I'd have told you myself. I don't want to lie any more. It's true: I have a lover! I love him! I want to live with him, do you understand?

Serpieri clutches his wife's arm. The door opens and a woman appears. Ussoni and another patriot are in the room.

WOMAN: Oh, Livia, at last! We've been waiting for you. Come in, come in!

Ussoni comes up to Livia with outstretched arms.

USSONI: Livia! Livia! What joy, at last!

Serpieri follows Livia in.

SERPIERI: It's you! I didn't know you were back! You could have let me know!

The woman closes the door. Livia is overcome by emotion and takes refuge in Ussoni's arms.

USSONI: Livia, we were able to get across the border last night. *(Music ends.)* I have to get in touch with our friends here in Venice. There's not a minute to lose, and the situation being what it is...

SERPIERI: Why didn't you trust me? She... tried to make me believe that...

LIVIA: You can't understand! You can't understand!

Ussoni leads the woman toward the center of the room.

SERPIERI: I've already spoken to Livia... very clearly. *(They walk into the adjoining room.)* Now I'll tell you yourself what I told her. *(A dozen patriots are busy with pamphlets, pistols, etc.)* I have absolutely no intention of accepting the responsibilities that the Austrian command has recently offered me, with very great insistence.

One of the patriots comes up to Livia.

LOREDAN: Livia, hello. How are you?

SERPIERI: I'm a Venetian born and bred, and you know perfectly well that all my interests and affections lie in this city. Now it's obvious that whichever way the war ends, Venice will certainly go to the Italian government. The French emperor has guaranteed that.

As Serpieri speaks, some of the patriots are taking inventory of the donations that the Italians have made for the partisan volunteers. Their words are barely audible.

PATRIOT: A gold pin with two stones. Twenty-five florins. A silver snuffbox. Two gold medals. A diamond pin. A gold crucifix. A gold chain with a medal. A ring.

SERPIERI: And this is why I want to help you. You... can trust me. As you see, this is a very practical proposal and has nothing to do with passions or ideals or dreams that I do not share.

USSONI: I understand. And what do you expect in return?

SERPIERI: I've already told you... to be able to stay in my own city without trouble, whatever happens.

USSONI: I can't promise you anything.

SERPIERI: Certainly; but some day you could testify on my behalf.

Ussoni walks over to Livia, who is standing by the table where Loredan is taking inventory.

LOREDAN: A gold watch and chain...

USSONI: Livia, could you be ready to leave for Aldeno tomorrow?

SERPIERI: That's precisely what I want to do. I've been telling Livia for days now...

LIVIA: Yes, I've been putting it off. I wanted to wait for you... I was sure you'd come back.

USSONI: All right, Livia. But now there's no time to lose. I'll be leaving Venice, too, tomorrow. I have to try to get to the Italian army headquarters. They'll give me instructions for the volunteer troops. The liaison has been organized fairly well, as I'll explain. Luca's already at Aldeno. I'll be there soon, too, in four or five days, if all goes well. Meanwhile you'll have to bring along the money that's been collected. Give it to me, Andrea. *(Ussoni takes a bag of money and shows it to Livia.)* They need it right away. Our volunteers are living on charity, like beggars. It's a good sum of money. You must have helped collect it, too.

LIVIA: No.

Music begins. Livia moves a few steps toward the rear of the room and sits down on one of the cases stacked against the wall. Ussoni comes over to her and sits beside her.

USSONI: We've been waiting so long for this moment, and now that it's come... it almost seems as if we've been taken by surprise, doesn't it? It's frightening. *(A patriot approaches and hands Ussoni a little case.)* Each of us must behave as if the lives of all those who are fighting depended upon us. *(He hands the case on to Livia.)* We haven't any rights any more, Livia, only duties. We must forget ourselves, Livia. I'm not afraid of sounding rhetorical. Italy's at war. It's our war... our revolution.

The music ends.

The countryside near the Serpieri villa at Aldeno.

LIVIA'S VOICE: Roberto's words... his trust... gave me the courage to leave Venice. The first few quiet days we spent at our villa at Aldeno seemed to me like the period of convalescence that follows a violent childhood illness.

Livia's bedroom at the villa.

The furious barking of dogs continues throughout the scene. Livia is sleeping in the great bed. Someone knocks at the door. Livia stirs in her sleep.

VOICE OF WATCHMAN: Laura! Laura!

LAURA'S VOICE: Yes, I'm coming, just a minute. Keep your voice down.

VOICE OF WATCHMAN: Up on the balcony, when the dogs began barking... I saw him. The window's open.

LAURA'S VOICE: I didn't hear anything... Quiet, I said... The countess is sleeping.

Livia awakens.

LIVIA: Who is it?

LAURA'S VOICE: It's me, Laura.

LIVIA: What's going on?

LAURA'S VOICE: Please forgive me, Countess, but the watchman says...

Livia sits up in bed.

LIVIA: Yes!

She looks toward the window.

LAURA'S VOICE: They've seen someone on the balcony.

Livia looks around fearfully. Repeated knocks on the door. She gets up and slowly approaches the window.

LAURA'S VOICE: Madame! Madame!

Livia sees Franz on the balcony outside the window.

LIVIA: Ah!

Franz immediately enters the room. Livia tries to dominate the situation.

LAURA'S VOICE: They say they've seen someone on the balcony!

LIVIA: Yes, it was I! *(She turns toward Franz.)* You're mad!

FRANZ: I went mad in Venice, when you left. Is the door locked?

Livia shakes her head and runs toward the door.

LIVIA: Laura!

LAURA'S VOICE: Yes, madame.

LIVIA: I was on the balcony myself. Go on back to bed.

LAURA'S VOICE: See, stupid? Waking people up...

Livia locks the door.

FRANZ: Did they see me?

She turns quickly to Franz.

LIVIA: What mad idea is this? Eh? How did you get here?

Livia wraps herself in a great shawl. Franz takes off his cap and throws it on a chair. The servants are heard calling as they look for the man spotted on Livia's balcony.

FRANZ: What do you keep all those dogs for? To protect your-self from enemies or from lovers?

LIVIA: Why did you decide to come here, Franz?

Livia, extremely agitated, crosses the room to lean on the baseboard of the bed.

FRANZ: I didn't decide anything; I came. I suddenly needed to see you and I came. *(He comes over to Livia and clutches her arm.)* Livia! Livia!

She frees herself. Franz comes up behind her. The voices of the servants and the barking of the dogs grow louder.

FRANZ: So I'm to be torn to pieces by your dogs?

He starts to turn toward the window. Livia stops him, clutching his shoulders.

LIVIA: No, no, no, no! No, go... go there and hide. *(She points to a corner of the room.)* Go, go, go! There!

Franz goes. Livia runs back to the window on the balcony. She closes the shutters and returns. Music begins.

LIVIA: I... I don't believe you've risked your life just to see me. Once I would have believed you... before you began to miss all those appointments... before those terrible days... when I could not find you.

Livia is sitting on the bed. Franz is seen behind the tulle curtains, leaning against the wall.

FRANZ: I'm younger than you are, Countess Serpieri, and not as clever as I'd like to think. When I began to realize I'd fallen in love... with a woman who could never love me...

LIVIA: Ah!

FRANZ: I could think of nothing better to do than disappear. That's why you didn't see me again. But it didn't work. When I found you were the one who was avoiding me... *(He slowly approaches Livia and kneels before her.)* ...that you'd left Venice... I could think of only one thing: to find you again!

LIVIA: You must have some reason. I can't yet understand.

FRANZ: What other reason would a man risk his neck for to come here?

LIVIA: Don't you realize? We're at war now!

FRANZ: War? *(He buries his head in her lap.)* Ah, I'm so tired. I only want to look at you, be with you. That's what I've come for. I've come... and I think of nothing else.

LIVIA: Once... I might have believed you.

Livia rises and walks forward. Franz remains sitting next to the bed.

FRANZ: Well, if you don't believe me I'd better leave right now.

LIVIA: No! Wait... wait.

The music ends. Franz smiles in triumph and then laughs loudly.

LIVIA: Franz... come here, Franz! *(She walks toward him.)* Franz, stay here!

FRANZ: Here? All right!

LIVIA: Please... don't make any noise. Please... wait...

She picks up a lighted lamp and walks out, motioning to Franz to be quiet. She closes the door. Two maids are walking up the outside stairway of Villa Serpieri, followed by a stable boy.

STABLE BOY: There're thieves in the garden, thieves!

Livia appears at the top of the stairs, holding the lighted lamp.

MAID: Madame!

SECOND MAID: Madame, what's happening?

Livia goes back inside, followed by two dogs.

LIVIA: Quiet, idiot.

A bell rings. Livia enters the drawing room, followed by the gardener. She walks toward the great center table.

LAURA: Ah, madame, madame, what a scare! I felt uneasy all night long; I couldn't sleep. But was it really you on the balcony?

Serpieri is leaning out of a window overlooking the garden.

SERPIERI: Simone! Be sure to look everywhere! Try to find some tracks!

The back lawn of Villa Serpieri.

In the rear, peasants with lanterns and leashed dogs are searching for the intruder.

PEASANT: Yes! Here the gravel's all messed up!

SERPIERI: Be sure no one's hiding in the garden!

PEASANT: Yes, sir.

SERPIERI: All right. *(Livia stands by the table in the drawing room; Laura closes the entrance door.)* Simone, keep on searching with the dogs!

Livia picks up the lamp from the table and starts back to her apartment; Laura follows her.

LAURA: Will you need me, madame?

Livia stops.

LIVIA: No. I don't need anything. Go, go to bed.

Livia goes out.

SERPIERI: Keep on looking. He must have run off when the dogs began barking. *(After Livia closes the door, Laura goes up to it as if to spy on her.)* I'm going back to bed.

SERVANT: Good night, sir.

Livia sits at her dressing table, passing her hands over her face and evidently exhausted. The calls of the count and the peasants filter through from the garden.

FRANZ: I'm sorry. You must forgive me.

The dressing-table mirror reflects Franz's image holding one of Livia's veils in his hands.

LIVIA: We're not in Venice anymore. I've changed now. I can think again and I am as clearheaded as I used to be.

Franz approaches her.

FRANZ: Livia, listen...

LIVIA: No, we're not in Venice anymore.

Franz circles the dressing table, still watching Livia, who does not look at him.

LIVIA: You were able to make me forget all my decency, all my dignity!

FRANZ: But why?

LIVIA: Yes, it's true, all my dignity... for a sad and guilty love... that could only shame me.

Franz bends over her. He caresses her shoulder.

FRANZ: Livia, my love...

LIVIA: We're not in Venice.

FRANZ: All right; we're not in Venice. We're agreed on that at least. *(He moves away.)* May I sit down?

LIVIA: Yes. You can't go... until they tie up the dogs.

FRANZ: Thanks.

Livia is still seated at the dressing table. Franz comes up to her, takes off his cape and throws it on a sofa.

FRANZ: I'm so sleepy. I haven't slept for three days. *(He lies down wearily on the dormeuse.)* I like the smell of summer... I like the smell of fresh-cut wheat. This place is full of that smell. I'm so exhausted! There's such a lazy smell in the air! *(He lifts himself up a bit and leans toward Livia.)* What did you say? Did you say something?

LIVIA: The dogs have gone away.

FRANZ: You... talk so softly... I can't understand what you say. I misunderstood you. I thought you said... you said... Franz... dear Franz... I'm so lonely. Please... stay with me.

LIVIA: You misunderstood.

FRANZ: I'm sorry. *(Franz lies down again.)* I misunderstood.

LIVIA: I said you must go now. You must go, you must go.

FRANZ: What did you say?

LIVIA: I said... the danger's past. You can go.

FRANZ: How long... how long it's been since we've seen each other, my love! I dreamed that you'd tell me...

LIVIA: I said go away. Go, go, go, go, go.

FRANZ: Is that really what you want? I hoped you'd ask me to stay.

Franz rises and approaches Livia. Livia feels Franz standing behind her.

LIVIA: Oh! Oh, Franz... Franz. Franz. *(Livia rises to his embrace.)* Yes, Franz... *(They kiss.)* ...please, stay.

The little lamp on the table next to Livia's bed slowly goes out. Livia and Franz, lying on the sofa, are reflected in the mirror. Franz's head lies in her lap; he is asleep. Livia looks at the window and caresses his hair.

LIVIA: It's almost dawn... and you told me you have to be in Verona before night.

Franz stirs and turns.

FRANZ: Who is it? Who is it?

LIVIA: It's me, Livia. Franz, wake up, it's dawn.

FRANZ: What did you say?

LIVIA: You must go right away. The sun will be up soon. And if they see you...

FRANZ: Close your eyes.

LIVIA: I haven't closed them all night.

FRANZ: Why not?

LIVIA: I was watching you as you slept.

Franz raises himself up and kisses Livia on the neck.

FRANZ: That's why I slept so well. I dreamed I was home. I was a little boy playing soldier with a wooden sword.

Franz laughs and kisses Livia's mouth and hands. He pulls her to him and they kiss again. Still kissing, they rise. Then Franz looks out the window.

FRANZ: I have to go.

LIVIA: Oh, I wish you would stay. I wish... I could...

FRANZ: What do you wish, sweetheart?

LIVIA: I wish I could lie in your arms as I did tonight... for our whole lives.

They kiss again.

FRANZ: Farewell. I must go, I must go.

He pulls away from her.

LIVIA: No!

FRANZ: The sun is about to rise, it's already very late. You don't want them to see me climbing down from your window, do you?

LIVIA: No, no! No, not yet! I'll hide you. I'll have you with me... one more day. Wait! Wait!

The attic of Villa Serpieri, now used as a granary. The two lovers enter one of the rooms and go through a pair of doors into a third room.

LIVIA: Come, quick!

They walk hand in hand over the grain. A bell rings the hour. Franz stops, lays his cape in the grain, and kneels down on it. Livia joins him after glancing out the window.

FRANZ: Livia! *(Franz reaches out and takes her hands in his own. Livia sits beside him.)* Come here! Stay here a little while.

LIVIA: No, no, the maid must find me in my room.

FRANZ: But it's still early. There's time.

LIVIA: Shh! Don't talk so loud!

FRANZ: I won't say another word. *(He lies down, propped up on his elbow.)* You know, it's comfortable here. I could stay here the rest of my life.

LIVIA: Then why don't you stay?

FRANZ: Did you forget, I have to go fight, be a hero?

LIVIA: Oh no... no! Try to forget!

FRANZ: I wish one could forget! A friend of mine did something incredible.

LIVIA: Who?

FRANZ: Another fellow. *(Franz turns over, lying on the cape.)* An officer.

LIVIA: What did he do?

FRANZ: He was able to bribe a doctor and get himself declared unfit for military service. He went for an examination, understand? *(Livia's hand caresses Franz's shoulder.)* And the doctor had agreed to find he had a heart ailment... that called for a calm, restful type of life. *(Livia's face nears Franz's.)* So they sent him home free.

LIVIA: Is it possible?

FRANZ: I just told you so, didn't I? He paid off the doctor. It took a lot of money. I didn't think that kind of thing could happen. But, after all, our generation has been spoiled,

like children. We like elegant uniforms because they make us look good! The gold epaulets, the ribbons, the sound of the band... that plays as we go off to be heroes. But there's the other side of the·coin. No women. Hunger. Cold. Exhaustion. Yes, we're all eager as long as it's only a matter of toasting our future victories, but we don't feel up to paying the price for what those victories often cost... the loss of an arm...*(Livia draws back in horror.)* A leg amputated at the hip...

LIVIA: Stop it!

FRANZ: ...a face disfigured so badly that people are horrified!

LIVIA: No, Franz, no, no!

Franz laughs.

FRANZ: Why? That's war! Tens of thousands of men ready to kill each other, for no reason, for no purpose. Reason has nothing to do with war. *(He laughs again.)* What is war, anyway, but a convenient way to make men think and act as best suits those who command them? *(Livia, terrorized, leans against one of the uprights of the granary.)* Why don't you say something, dear? What are you thinking about?

LIVIA: It's horrible! War's horrible! *(She moves a few steps away. Franz follows her with his eyes.)* I'll come back as soon as I can.

She moves away and walks out.

The road leading uphill toward the villa.

There is a continual passage of Austrian troops and supply carts. Serpieri is talking with his overseer.

OVERSEER: So many of them passed by last night! The heavy artillery too. The whole house shook! They're coming from Innsbruck and going down to Verona.

SERPIERI: They're going to Verona.

The gardener comes up to them.

GARDENER: Sir!

SERPIERI: Yes!

GARDENER: Sir, do you want me to report what happened last night to the police?

SERPIERI: No, better not. I'll bet it was someone looking for the grain... to try to get us into trouble.

OVERSEER: But the men haven't said a word for sure. They all stand to benefit.

SERPIERI: Anyway the best thing to do is put a watchman out at night. *(Serpieri points to a spot in the distance.)* But... but look over there! Isn't that the Ronghe! It's at the Ronghe!

(He moves off, followed by the overseer and the gardener; Livia is in the middle of the garden.) That fire over there!

OVERSEER: It's at the Ronghe! That's a fire, and a big one too!

SERPIERI: Let's go see!

They leave.

GARDENER'S VOICE: Look... look, sir, what thick black smoke down there. Seems like a haystack on fire!

Laura approaches Livia and hands her a shawl. A bell rings the alarm.

SERPIERI'S VOICE: We have to send someone right away, there isn't a minute to lose!

GARDENER'S VOICE: To the Ronghe! To the Ronghe!

Serpieri, the gardener, and the overseer run toward the garden wall in the direction of the column of thick black smoke visible in the distance.

GARDENER: It's at Mangini's house.

SERPIERI: No, it can't be at Mangini's, it's behind the hill. It's further off.

Livia runs up to the group.

OVERSEER: It's most likely Piovene's stables.

Serpieri turns upon hearing Livia.

SERPIERI: Come, let's go look from the attic.

LIVIA: They must be burning the underbrush.

GARDENER: But don't you see, ma'am, it's a column of smoke. It must be Mangini's house.

LIVIA: You're right; we can see it fine from here. Maybe it's an army camp.

SERPIERI: We'd better make sure. *(Serpieri moves off.)* Come on with me, you two. *(The overseer and the gardener follow. Livia glances worriedly at the attic window, then runs after them.)*

The three men go up the steps leading to the attic.

SERPIERI: That's all we needed. Let's look out the windows!

Livia follows them some steps behind.

GARDENER: Let's hope the wind doesn't shift, because with all the hay stacked in the shed...

SERPIERI: Let's hope, let's hope!

They reach the granary. The gardener runs to a window.

GARDENER: Can you hear the Ronghe bells, sir?

SERPIERI: Yes. It's about time. What were they waiting for? That the whole town should go up in flames first?

Livia appears on the second flight of stairs leading up to the granary.

GARDENER: You can't see anything from here, sir. Let's try the other side.

A moment later, Livia comes up the last few steps. Serpieri, the gardener, and the overseer are trying to force open the door leading to the third room of the granary.

SERPIERI: What's going on here? It's been locked!

Livia appears as the overseer disappears up a stairway leading to the dormer windows.

OVERSEER'S VOICE: The grain's blocking it, sir.

Finally the door gives way and the group, along with the overseer who races back down the stairs, rushes into the room. Livia leans against the wall near the door, in extreme agitation.

GARDENER'S VOICE: You can see fine from here! Sir, let's hope no fighting's broken out between the Austrians and the patriots camped at Romagnano! You know, sometimes, to get revenge...

SERPIERI'S VOICE: Where are they camped? *(Livia races to the door of the third room.)* Near the villages? But that's insane. It puts everybody in danger.

GARDENER'S VOICE: They're not so near! But sometimes, sir... *(Their voices are audible but the words cannot be well distinguished.)* ...they go there for supplies.

SERPIERI'S VOICE: And for that our farms are burned! *(Livia, by the door, walks a few steps forward.)* Antonio!

SERVANT'S VOICE: Yes, sir!

Livia enters the room. The servant runs to the window where the count and the others are watching the fire.

SERPIERI: Go get Giuseppe!

SERVANT: Yes, sir.

The servant runs off. But at the center of the room he is stopped by the voice of the count.

SERPIERI: Oh! Antonio! *(Coming up to him)* You'd better tell him to hitch up the horses to the carriage. Hurry! Hurry!

SERVANT: Yes, sir.

The servant passes in front of Livia and glances at her curiously. The men in the granary continue to talk very excitedly.

Livia enters the drawing room of the villa.

LAURA: Madame... madame...

LIVIA: What is it?

LAURA: That person... is in there... and Luca's come too, from Romagnano.

Luca comes up from the rear of the drawing room.

LUCA: Hello, Countess Serpieri. There's good news. Marquis Ussoni has gotten through to the Italian headquarters on the Mincio. Now it's just a matter of hours. Our orders should come through any time now. Garibaldi's at Salò. Two of our representatives met with one of his officers yesterday at Trent. General Garibaldi sent a message praising the patriots. He didn't know we had so many men. You'll see, ma'am, when the Italian troops get here they'll find the whole job all wound up. We'll free our land ourselves without anybody's help.

LIVIA: Yes, yes, of course. You'll tell me everything later on. Come back later. *(Livia turns and walks away from Luca.)* Maybe this evening.

LUCA: Countess, Marquis Ussoni sent word too that you were to give me the money that was collected in Venice. It should be more than three thousand florins.

LIVIA: I don't know. I haven't checked. It's probably as you say. This evening, I said, come back this evening, all right?

SERPIERI'S VOICE: Anyway, I say that to... *(Serpieri enters the drawing room, followed by the overseer and the gardener. They come toward the center of the room.)* ...get to that stage takes time. And of course no one gives you any warning, or tells you anything. Not a single word. I may be a fool but...

A servant runs up to the count.

SERVANT: Sir, Giuseppe's hitching up now, sir; it'll be ready in a minute.

SERPIERI: Good!

OVERSEER: I'll go, sir!

SERPIERI: Yes, and try to hurry.

The overseer runs out.

OVERSEER'S VOICE: Giuseppe! Giuseppe! Giuseppe!

LUCA: Hello, sir.

SERPIERI: Hello. Antonio, my hat! *(Serpieri walks out; his voice continues off-camera.)* Quick! Antonio! I'm in a hurry!

Laura is leaving but Livia stops her.

LIVIA: Show Luca out!

Luca moves toward the door.

LUCA: Goodbye, Countess!

LIVIA: Till this evening!

LUCA: All right, Countess.

When the two have gone out, Livia goes to the center of the room, then suddenly changes her mind and walks back.

Livia runs to the door of the guest room. Franz is eating breakfast.

LIVIA: How did you get here?

FRANZ: Laura! Isn't that her name? Your maid! I thought you'd sent... She's extraordinary. She came to get me, brought me here, and gave me breakfast.

Livia hurries to close the curtains of one of the windows.

LIVIA: My God! *(She goes to another window.)* So she knows you're here.

FRANZ: So what? That's what ladies' maids are for.

Livia closes the last curtain. Laura appears in the doorway.

LAURA: Madame, the master's looking for you!

Livia looks for a moment at Franz and then runs out.

Livia at the top of the stairs.

Serpieri is about to get into a small carriage driven by the overseer.

SERPIERI: We're leaving. Don't wait for me for lunch.

LIVIA: All right.

SERPIERI: What?

LIVIA: I said all right.

Serpieri gets into the carriage and it races off.

OVERSEER: My respects, ma'am.

LIVIA: Goodbye.

The carriage goes off along the graveled drive to the gate. Music begins. Livia watches the carriage drive off and then walks back into the house.

As she appears in the doorway, Franz moves smilingly out from behind the curtain where he has been concealed. They embrace and kiss.

Livia is seated at the foot of the bed with her head leaning on one hand. Franz comes over to her and sits down beside her.

FRANZ: What are you thinking about?

LIVIA: I was thinking... something.

FRANZ: Tell me what.

LIVIA: This morning, up in the granary, you told me about that friend of yours... who was sent home because a doctor declared he had a heart ailment.

FRANZ: So?

Livia takes Franz's hand and kisses it.

LIVIA: Couldn't you do the same thing?

FRANZ: Who, me?

LIVIA: Yes, Franz, you.

FRANZ: You want me to play cripple? And bribe that rascal and pass for sick?

LIVIA: Yes.

FRANZ: You... you... think I'm capable of such a vile thing? And even if it's vile it... takes a lot of money.

LIVIA: How much?

The music ends. Franz rises and walks up and down the room. Then he stops, fiddling with his suspenders.

FRANZ: Two thousand florins.

LIVIA: Two thousand florins! Impossible!

Livia rises. Franz goes over to her.

FRANZ: That's more than I'm worth?

LIVIA: If only I could! If there were some way! You could stay here near me... perhaps at Trent, couldn't you?

FRANZ: No. No. The regulations say that a soldier on sick leave has to stay near his own regiment all the same.

Livia leaves Franz and goes toward the fireplace, desperately clutching her head in her hands.

LIVIA: Oh, Franz, Franz! Oh, Franz... if only I could!

Franz takes his jacket and cap from the table.

FRANZ: I must go; it's late!

LIVIA: Oh no! No!

FRANZ: If I don't get to Verona by tomorrow morning they'll declare me a deserter.

LIVIA: Nooo!

She clutches his shoulders.

FRANZ: I could be shot... and that would be the end of all our problems.

LIVIA: No!

FRANZ: Time's run out!

LIVIA: Wait... wait, Franz... Wait!

Music begins. Livia leaves Franz and goes to the door. She turns, then crosses the anteroom, opens one door and then another. Franz follows her. Livia comes back to the sitting room with a little casket. She sets it down on a desk and then looks at Franz.

LIVIA: Close that door! Come here. *(Franz rapidly closes the door.)* Quick!

He runs to Livia. She has taken a bag full of coins from the casket. Franz picks up a handful.

FRANZ: Is it yours?

LIVIA: No, no!

FRANZ: Your husband's?

LIVIA: No, no!

FRANZ: Then whose is it?

Livia turns and sits down on a hassock. As she does so, she unintentionally sweeps the florins over the desk and onto the floor.

LIVIA: I can't tell you. You'll think I'm mad! And I am! I'm mad!

She buries her head in her hands and sobs desperately. Franz kneels before her and puts his head in her lap, quickly gathering up the coins from the floor with one hand.

FRANZ: Oh, my love! My love! My love! My poor... desperate love! Sweetheart! Sweetheart! My poor poor girl! My poor desperate love!

Someone knocks on the door.

LIVIA: Who is it?

LAURA'S VOICE: It's me, madame. May I come in?

Livia rises and goes to the door.

LIVIA: Don't come in! *(Laura knocks again.)* Don't come in!

LAURA'S VOICE: But it's me, madame!

LIVIA: Don't come in, I tell you! *(Livia turns to Franz.)* Did you count it? *(She runs to him.)* Do you think it's enough?

FRANZ: Livia, I know you've given me your heart... and not only your heart. *(Franz embraces her.)* I don't feel guilty... accepting it. I'd feel guilty not to accept it. Can you believe me?

Laura knocks again. Livia breaks away from Franz.

LAURA'S VOICE: Madame, madame. *(The music ends; Livia opens the door and Laura appears.)* Madame, I think the count is coming back!

LIVIA: Oh, yes, all right, I understand.

Laura runs across the room and hands Franz his cape and cap.

LAURA: Tonio saw him in the village a little while ago, and he told him...

LIVIA: Yes, yes.

LAURA: I told Tonio to wait in the kitchen. And I've had the gardener called too with some excuse. *(Laura makes Franz move away and then turns to Livia.)* You mustn't go by the terrace... because Ada's taking in the laundry. I tried to call her inside, but... then Luca came. I've put him in

the drawing room... *(Livia, who has been writing a note in the meanwhile, turns to Laura.)* ...and he's waiting there.

LIVIA: Yes.

Livia folds the note and walks away. Laura has noticed the florins scattered over the floor, and after glancing about warily, she hurries to pick them up.

Livia and Franz walk along a corridor. Leaning against the wall, Laura watches them go off. Music begins.

Livia and Franz face each other.

LIVIA: Write as soon as you can. Don't forget. *(She takes the note she has just written from her sleeve.)* I've written the address here. Have some civilian take the letter to Luca. He'll get it right away. I must know.

FRANZ: Yes, yes. I'll write.

LIVIA: Remember... as soon as you can. *(They kiss.)* Go now. Tell me when everything's set. I'll come to you right away. I can't go on living like this.

FRANZ: You shouldn't love me. *(He turns and starts to go, then stops to look at Livia for a moment.)* No one should.

He races away with his white cape flying behind. At the corner he stops a moment, then disappears.

LIVIA'S VOICE: I was tied to him forever now. For his sake I'd forgotten... betrayed the men who were fighting. *(She turns back along the corridor, leaning against the wall.)* I was trying to make my dreams come true, to end my suffering.

Music ends.

Courtyard of the Italian army headquarters.

General Sirtori's party enters at a gallop: two Aosta lancer couriers, the general's carriage, and the escort of lancers. The carriage races through the courtyard, where the men have snapped to attention, and halts abruptly at the entrance to headquarters.

Ussoni, standing in front of the entrance, walks toward the gate. A bugler sounds the "At Ease" and the men begin to move about again in the court-yard.

CAPTAIN MEUCCI: Marquis Ussoni! *(Hearing his name called, Ussoni stops; Captain Meucci comes up to him.)* I advise you to get to Oliosi, keeping away from the left wing of our forces just outside Valeggio. But I warn you, it'll be difficult to get through.

Ussoni takes off his hat.

USSONI: Thanks!

He walks off.

MEUCCI: Good luck, Marquis Ussoni.

A patrol of lancers and two military carts cross a bridge where some grenadiers in campaign uniform are leaning against the rail. Ussoni crosses the bridge. Several quartermaster troops are busy slaughtering a calf. Singing begins.

A gig appears, driven by a young peasant. Ussoni raises his hand to stop him.

USSONI: Halt! Stop! I have to get to Oliosi, near Montevento. Can you take me?...

PEASANT: It's dangerous.

USSONI: Don't worry about that. We can try another road. *(A squad of grenadiers comes up, marching under an officer's command; Ussoni takes some coins from a purse and hands them to the peasant.)* Here. Take this!

He jumps up onto the gig next to the peasant, who picks up the reins and departs.

A column of military carts passes near the Visconteo bridge. Ussoni's gig drives alongside the column. A hay cart coming along in the opposite direction blocks the road. Ussoni's gig, in the center of the confusion, is barely able to get through.

A patrol of guides gallops toward a patrol of Aosta lancers. Some peasants climb up onto two hay carts. Three horse-drawn artillery pieces appear galloping toward the river.

The threshing-floor in front of a farmhouse.

The peasants are intent on their customary tasks as groups of soldiers rest nearby. Ussoni's gig appears and draws up before an officer.

USSONI: Lieutenant, what's the best way... *(Ussoni, on the gig, shows the lieutenant a topographical map.)* ...to get to Oliosi?

LIEUTENANT: Oliosi? But the roads to Montevento are all blocked. There's fighting going on. *(The lieutenant points to a road.)* Try to get to that hill. Turn left. You'll see a large farm-house. It's called Ca' Pasquàl.

Ussoni checks the map.

USSONI: Yes, here it is.

LIEUTENANT: All right. From there you keep going down toward your left.

PASINI: And there's the road to Maragnote and we go down to Menso.

USSONI: Here, fine. So we circle around and get to Sant'Ambrogio all the same. Thanks, lieutenant, thanks a lot. You're from the South?

LIEUTENANT: Naples.

USSONI: Good luck, lieutenant.

LIEUTENANT: Thanks!

Ussoni shakes the lieutenant's hand cordially.

USSONI: Give me the reins, I'll drive now.

Ussoni takes the reins and changes places with the peasant.

PEASANT: Yes, sir! But go slow!

Ussoni's gig leaves the threshing area.

Ussoni's gig reaches a large farmhouse which has been requisitioned by a medical unit. Artillery is audible in the distance. A cart full of wounded troops enters the farmyard. Two medical aides run forward with a stretcher.

Ussoni's gig continues down the road, where several medical aides are tending the wounded. The gig drives away as we see a camp with tents, horses, field kitchen, carts, etc. Grenades are exploding everywhere. Ussoni's gig drives forward and stops.

USSONI: I have to get to the other side of the hill. *(A soldier answers; the words are inaudible.)* But I've got to get through! I have a pass, signed by General La Marmora himself. Here...

A voice shouts, "To arms!" A bugler and an officer run forward and stop.

OFFICER: To arms!

The bugler sounds the call. On the left is a field with shocks of wheat standing in rows; each shock conceals a soldier. At the call they race out. The officers run to lead the charge. The soldiers fix bayonets. The flag bearer appears; he takes the flag from its case and unfurls it to the wind.

The soldiers advance slowly. Grenades explode and clouds of smoke cover the battlefield. Shots, bugle calls, shouts. A large group of soldiers charges forward behind its flag. Ussoni's carriage gallops along a road, almost running into a platoon of Austrian dragoons charging down the hill to attack the Italians.

Villa Serpieri.

Livia walks slowly along under the portico. A maid follows a short distance behind her.

LIVIA'S VOICE: I'd received a letter from Franz. He'd been exempted... and was in Verona. But he begged me not to come. *(Music begins; Livia stops, gazing at the horizon, then turns and walks back.)* He was afraid of the danger. The fighting had

begun along the whole front, and at Aldeno we heard that the Italians had been victorious, as had been expected.

Music ends. A peasant appears at the end of the portico.

PEASANT: You can see the cannons shooting from Sant'Ambrogio. They're near here.

WATCHMAN: I told you the Germans'd get out of Verona!

SECOND SERVANT: No, they already left yesterday!

WATCHMAN: This time we'll be rid of these Germans for good.

Another peasant runs up to where the others are standing on the threshing floor.

PEASANT: Quiet, I see Luca coming.

Luca enters the gate and comes up the drive, followed by several peasants and servants.

PEASANTS: Here's Luca. Quiet, let's hear what he says! Here he comes. What did he say? The Germans have left Verona! We'll get 'em all! Hurrah for Italy!

A peasant unfurls an Italian flag. Livia comes up to the group.

PEASANT: They've left Verona!

LUCA: Hello, Countess.

LIVIA: Who... who says the Austrians are leaving Verona?

Luca comes up to Livia.

LUCA: Yes, ma'am, because it seems the Italians are advancing along the whole front, and the Austrians have asked for reinforcements even from Trent. *(Livia sits down on a bench standing against the stable wall; another peasant appears.)*

LUCA: And it seems they're leaving Verona too.

FIRST PEASANT: They won't stop at Verona this time. They'll throw them all out. They'll drive them into the sea.

Another peasant appears carrying an Italian flag.

SECOND PEASANT: Hurrah for Italy, ma'am, hurrah for Italy!

LIVIA: But will we be cut off?

LUCA: This is the moment for us to act. Marquis Ussoni...

LIVIA: We haven't heard a thing about him. No news. Nothing. *(Music begins.)* We can't act. We have to wait for orders.

LUCA: But Countess, we can't wait any more. Even if communications are cut off, our volunteers have to get into it and occupy the area. There's not a moment to lose.

LIVIA: We'll be cut off.

LUCA: We'll have Garibaldi here!

SECOND PEASANT: Countess... Garibaldi... for God's sake!

Livia pulls her shawl around her. The music ends.

A country road hit by the war.

Wounded and exhausted soldiers pass by. The defeat of the Italian army is obvious.

Sound of artillery and rifles. Two medical carts stand in a meadow; nuns and medical aides are tending the wounded. Ussoni comes up the road, trying to find someone to question.

USSONI: What's going on? What are you doing? *(No one answers him; he stops an army officer.)* What's going on, lieutenant? Where are you going?

LIEUTENANT: We've been ordered to retreat.

As Ussoni goes toward the rear, the lieutenant follows the column of carts, cannon, and soldiers in retreat. The corpses of the dead lie beside the road.

Ussoni suddenly leaves the road and heads toward the field where the fighting is still going on. Groups of soldiers begin to charge, and the

Austrian infantry races down a little hill. Ussoni is lost to view in the fighting.

Ussoni advances among abandoned cases of supplies and smoldering underbrush in an area of the battlefield still being contested. Sounds of battle. He is hit by an enemy bullet and almost falls, but pulls himself together, grits his teeth, and stumbles on, cradling his wounded arm with the good one.

Ussoni climbs up a crest atop which Italian soldiers are laboring around four cannons. A lieutenant exhorts them to resist.

LIEUTENANT: Come on! Come on! *(Ussoni, exhausted, sits on the ground; the lieutenant notices him.)* Who are you? Are you wounded?

USSONI: They're all retreating, lieutenant.

The sound of the guns covers part of the dialogue.

LIEUTENANT: Yes, it's true. It's a disaster. But we're not retreating. Right, boys?

A SOLDIER: Of course not!

ANOTHER SOLDIER: That's the truth. No one's leaving here.

An officer of the scouts rides up.

SCOUT LIEUTENANT: Orders to retreat!

LIEUTENANT: We're all retreating.

SCOUT: All right, lieutenant.

LIEUTENANT: Come on, boys!

Villa Serpieri.

Livia comes out and gets into a carriage.

LIVIA'S VOICE: I decided to leave... at dawn... before the area around Aldeno was occupied by the patriots... before the Italians could get to Verona. I knew I was leaving my home... and my people... forever. *(The carriage drives off; the gate is closed behind it as several servants and patriots watch curiously.)* And yet I felt no remorse or sadness.

Livia inside the carriage.

LIVIA'S VOICE: The carriage was burning hot, and I felt I was suffocating in that stuffy air. *(She takes one of Franz's letters from her purse; music begins.)* I had one of Franz's letters with me, and I read it over and over again, though I knew it by heart: "My beloved Livia... You have saved my life. The money was sufficient, at least for now, to fill the greedy bellies of the doctors. They've exempted me and kept me in Verona. I have a nice room overlooking the river, in Via Santo Stefano 149. It needs only your presence, day and night. But don't come now. Don't move. The trip would be too dangerous. Love me always as I love you."

Voices are heard outside, evidently of Austrian officers. Livia passes a handkerchief over her face, which is beginning to show signs of weariness.

The carriage drives through a Verona street.

Livia wipes her face again with the handkerchief. A great deal of dust enters the carriage. But the thought of meeting Franz shortly gives her courage and makes her smile with pleasure.

The carriage drives along the road. The music ends. Sound of soldiers.

The gates of Verona.

Austrian soldiers and carts are crowded before the gates. Livia's carriage appears and drives under the portico. Music begins. Two Austrian soldiers stop her at the check point.

OFFICER: Do you have a pass to go into Verona at this time of night?

LIVIA: No, but... I'm Countess Serpieri. My husband's an Austrian official. I've come to see some relatives in town.

OFFICER: *Sehr gut, gräfin.* You can go through. But I warn you that tonight the streets of Verona aren't very safe for a lady.

LIVIA: Thanks. Quick, Via Santo Stefano 149. Quick, move! Move!

COACHMAN: I'm going, ma'am.

The carriage moves through the crowd as the coachman shouts. Music ends.

The long hall leading to Franz's apartment.

Music begins. Livia walks along, keeping to the wall. She stops at a hall, exhausted and overcome with emotion. Then she runs to a door which she sweeps open with sudden resolution. She stops on the sill.

LIVIA: Franz! *(Livia runs across the room toward Franz, who is closing his bedroom door; the music stops.)* Franz!

Franz turns and looks at her with indifference.

FRANZ: Look what a nice surprise!

LIVIA: Oh, Franz!

FRANZ: What?

Livia takes a few steps toward Franz.

LIVIA: I'm here.

FRANZ: Has something happened?

LIVIA: I'm here, Franz.

Livia clutches his shoulder for a moment.

FRANZ: I wrote you not to come. *(He walks away from her; she follows him.)* Didn't you get the letter?

LIVIA: Yes, but I came all the same. I couldn't live with that terror any more.

FRANZ: What terror? Terror of what?

LIVIA: Of what might happen to you.

Livia puts her hand to his face to caress him, but he seizes it pitilessly.

FRANZ: You knew I was safe. And you knew why too. With your

money. *(He again walks away from her.)* You knew I'd bought myself safety, tranquillity, comfort, peace, pleasure...

Livia approaches him.

LIVIA: Oh, Franz. I wanted to be sure. *(She sits on a sofa.)* To see with my own eyes.

FRANZ: Well, now you've seen. You shouldn't have come here. You were wrong to do it and now you'll be sorry for it! Look, I'm not an officer any more. *(She rises and comes over to him.)* And not even a gentleman. *(Franz, a glass of wine in his hand, is standing by a table that has been laid for dinner.)* I'm a drunken deserter. *(He drinks and then throws the glass to the floor.)* What a stink! Turns one's stomach! *(Livia tries again to come to him, sobbing.)* Stink of cowardice and vice.

LIVIA: Now I'm here, Franz. I'll stay with you always. I've left everything for you. Take me in your arms, Franz!

FRANZ: I haven't washed or shaved for a few days. I don't want to turn your stomach by coming too close to you. *(He laughs softly.)* You'd get dirty.

He laughs more loudly, leaning with his hands against the wall. His laugh blends with his sobs of anger.

A woman's voice calls Franz.

CLARA'S VOICE: Franz! Franz! Oh, Franz!

Livia steps back. She bumps into something that crashes to the floor.

LIVIA: You're not alone?

FRANZ: She's not important. *(He crosses the room as if talking to himself.)* She comes every night to keep me company for a couple of hours. Want to meet her? *(Livia tries to retreat but Franz stops her with his hand.)* Don't be shy. After all, she belongs to you. I pay her with your money.

Livia runs across the room as Franz laughs like a madman. Something crashes to the ground as she passes by.

A girl appears in the bedroom doorway, lacing up her corset. Franz goes over to her.

FRANZ: Clara! Come here, Clara, come here! I want you to meet a great lady... Countess Livia Serpieri. She's just made a long trip. You can see how tired she is. She drove through the troops returning from battle... men who didn't have the good luck to have what I had... *(He closes the door, then speaks directly into Livia's face.)* A rich patroness! Clara, give her something to drink. *(Livia comes slowly over to the table and picks up a glass; music begins.)* And wash it first! Stupid! It's for a lady! *(Livia, breathing heavily, slowly walks over to an armchair.)* A lady doesn't drink from a dirty glass, don't you know that? *(Livia looks at Clara and seems about to collapse; Franz has followed her.)* Guests have to be properly treated.

Clara offers the glass to Livia.

CLARA: Don't you want it? Don't you feel well?

Livia walks away. The music ends. Franz approaches Clara.

FRANZ: What are you waiting for? Help her, idiot. *(Takes her by the shoulders and shakes her)* Take off her veil, come on, take off her hat and her gloves! Countess Serpieri's a real lady! She's an aristocrat, an important lady! Can't you see that? *(Franz comes toward Livia.)* She's an Italian aristocrat. I told you about her anyway.

CLARA: No.

FRANZ: Ah, you don't remember. You didn't listen because you thought I was just bragging. Ah, yes! You thought I was just bragging when I told you that a real lady like Countess Serpieri... *(He clutches Livia abruptly and pulls off her veil; music begins.)* ...had fallen in love with me. Really! She told me so herself. She'd never have known what love was if it hadn't been for me.

Livia's face is in desperate pain: humiliation, exhaustion, and anguished disillusion have aged her by many years. She is a defeated woman, no longer beautiful.

LIVIA: Why are you saying these things? To hurt me? To torture yourself?

FRANZ: Excuse me... *(The music ends.)* ...but I didn't hear you. You talk so softly. Did you hear what she said, Clara?

CLARA: No, I didn't hear anything. And I don't want to. I'm going.

FRANZ: But you're mad! Livia! *(He comes over to Livia.)* You absolutely cannot allow her to leave at this hour. Invite her to dine with us. Tell her!

Livia looks at the girl.

LIVIA: Please stay.

Franz smiles in triumph. He goes to the table. The girl sits down at the table.

CLARA: Don't pay any attention to him. He's drunk!

Livia approaches the table. Franz pushes her chair in as she sits down, then sits between the two women.

FRANZ: Just who do you think you are? You think you're too fine

to sit down with a whore? *(He pours himself some wine and drinks.)* What's the difference between you two? I'll tell you. She's young, and she's pretty. Men pay for her. While you... *(He laughs.)* Why are you looking at me that way? I don't like it, understand? You think I'm crazy? No, I'm not crazy. I've never been so sane in my life. *(He drinks again.)* Listen, and try to understand me. Try to see me as I really am, not the way you think I am. You've invented a perfectly fantastic idea of me. And it has nothing to do with the man I am. Who am I? How do I live? *(Music begins.)* On what? I get money in two ways. From women, and from cheating at cards. I'm a master at both. That's what I am. I have some other qualities too. I'm a deserter because I'm a coward. And I don't mind being either a deserter or a coward. What do I care if my compatriots have won a battle today at a place called Custoza... *(He turns to lean on the chair; his voice is breaking with emotion.)* ...when I know they'll lose the war. And not only the war. And in a few years Austria... will be finished. And a whole world will disappear. The one you and I belong to. And the new world your cousin talks of doesn't interest me. It's much better not to get involved in these things... and take one's pleasure where one finds it. *(He turns to Livia.)* And you believe that too, or else you wouldn't have given me money to buy an hour of love. *(The music ends; Livia sobs desperately; Franz beats his fist on the table.)* That's enough! *(Rises, holding his head in his hands)* It's too late; everything's finished. *(He walks away, then turns to Livia again.)* I'm not your romantic hero! And I don't love you any more. I wanted money, I got it, that's all! Oh, I forgot. I'm also... an informer. I was the one who denounced your cousin to the police. And of course you've always known it but you pretended not to, to save our love.

He laughs. Livia screams in exasperation.

LIVIA: No! *(She jumps up.)* No!

Franz continues to laugh. Livia runs to the armchair and takes her hat. Clara, in the background, watches the scene in terror. Livia takes her purse from the sofa and starts to leave.

FRANZ: Go, go, go, madame! Go, go, you whore! Go! *(Livia flings open the door and flees.)* Get out of here! Break your neck! Don't stop running!

Livia runs down the corridor, stopping now and then to lean against the wall. Franz can still be heard laughing.

Livia walks along a high wall in a Verona street. She meets a group of five drunken Austrians, who advance singing and laughing. One of them grabs her arm. Livia escapes and runs down the street.

Livia walks on. Drunken Austrians laugh, snicker, sing. Every now and then one of them grabs a woman, squeezes and kisses her. Couples enter a house. One soldier tries for a moment to stop Livia but immediately desists.

Livia leans against the wall by the stairway leading to the house, as soldiers and women pass by her to enter and leave.

Near the Austrian army headquarters.

Livia, exhausted, leans against a lamp post, then hurries along toward headquarters.

Livia enters the main drawing room of the headquarters building. A soldier invites her to sit down. An Austrian officer reads aloud the bulletin reporting the victory of Custoza. Several secretaries are working around a large table in the middle of the room.

Livia, who appears ever more exhausted, tries to rearrange her hair with one hand. The officer continues to read the bulletin.

Livia walks to the general's desk like an automaton.

LIVIA: I've come to do my duty as a faithful Austrian subject.

GENERAL: Ah! The countess is Austrian?

Livia shakes her head.

LIVIA: Venetian.

The general stands behind the desk. Almost disappointed by her answer, he sits down and looks at Livia. She takes a crumpled letter from her purse and throws it on the table.

LIVIA: Here!

The general picks up the letter and unfolds it, glancing rapidly at the first few lines.

GENERAL: I don't understand. The letter is addressed to you?

Livia nods; the general puts on his glasses, reads the first lines again, removes his glasses, and looks once more at Livia's address with an extremely serious expression. He rises suddenly and goes to close the door, through which his family is seen sitting around the dinner table. Then he turns abruptly to Livia.

GENERAL: Well, I'm in a hurry, what is it?

He approaches her. Music begins.

LIVIA: The letter was written by... Franz Mahler... of the Third Artillery.

GENERAL: So?

LIVIA: The letter's clear enough. He feigned illness and bribed the doctors. He's a deserter from the field of battle!

GENERAL: Ah, I understand. The lieutenant was your lover... and now you're taking your revenge by having him shot! Think twice, Countess! Informing is infamous! You're committing murder!

Livia closes her eyes, touched by the general's words, but she continues to be silent. The general throws the letter violently on the table and turns to the door.

GENERAL *(calling)* : Lieutenant Schneider!

Livia starts to leave; the general follows her with his eyes. At the doorway leading to the central hall, Livia leans against one of the doors as if to gather strength, then turns slightly toward the general.

LIVIA: General! Do your duty!

Lieutenant Schneider appears and comes to attention before the general.

The music ends.

GENERAL *(in German)* : Show the lady out!

The lieutenant leaves to carry out the order.

Stairway of the headquarters building. Austrian soldiers and officers come and go. Livia goes slowly up the stairs. An officer is shouting out orders in German from above.

OFFICER: See that this order is carried out immediately! *(The officer continues to shout out orders from the upper balcony.)* It is extremely urgent. You understand? Extremely urgent!

As Livia continues slowly down the stairs, an officer passes her with the order for Mahler's execution. The orders for Mahler's arrest continue to be shouted out in German.

OFFICER: It must be carried out immediately!

CORPORAL: The officer's order! The order! Arrest Lieutenant Franz Mahler immediately... living at Via Santo Stefano 149.

Livia reaches the great entrance door and goes out under the portico, where a platoon is forming up under the orders of an officer.

OFFICER OF THE DAY: Lieutenant Pirk!

LIEUTENANT PIRK: Yes!

OFFICER OF THE DAY: Arrest Lieutenant Franz Mahler, Via Santo Stefano 149, at once!

LIEUTENANT PIRK: Yes, sir!

The platoon commander gives several orders which the soldiers carry out, lining up by twos. Livia walks off. The platoon starts off. A soldier in the entranceway shouts.

SOLDIER: Corporal Kramer!

A Verona street. Music begins. Livia continues to walk aimlessly, passing by drunken soldiers singing to celebrate the victory.

Another Verona street.

Several exultant soldiers fire into the air. Livia approaches, staggering wearily. She brushes against the wall, barely managing to support her pain. Perhaps she has gone mad. Music ends.

LIVIA: Franz! Fraanz! Fraaanz!

Her shadow and the echo of her cries are lost in the night.

The Austrian squad designated to arrest Franz appears dragging him

along. He covers his face with his hands. Soldiers bearing torches lead the way. The platoon comes out from under an archway. Franz staggers. Drum roll begins. One of the soldiers prods him with his rifle butt.

Two soldiers hold Franz, almost carrying him bodily as he staggers along toward the execution field. The firing squad is already drawn up a few yards from the wall, under the command of an officer. The scene is lit by two squads of soldiers with torches. Two drummers are rolling their instruments ominously. A priest awaits the condemned man.

Franz Mahler is dragged roughly up against the wall by the two soldiers. His face is turned against the wall, his cape removed, and his eyes blindfolded. The priest gives him absolution. Then they all leave quickly as the first row of the firing squad kneels down to take aim. Off-camera singing.

Franz remains glued against the wall as they have left him, already almost a lifeless dummy.

SQUAD COMMANDER *(in German)* : Fire!

As the shots hit him, Franz twists around and falls to the ground. Drum roll ends. An officer runs to ascertain his death as the squad, once more in marching order, leaves at an officer's commands. The drums accompany the soldiers' marching.

Off-camera singing. Drum roll begins again. A group of soldiers picks up Franz's inanimate body and drags it away. The field is left empty. Drum roll ends.

Music begins. The credits appear superimposed on the field.

THE END.